SHOVELING
FUEL FOR A
RUNAWAY TRAIN

**UNIVERSITY OF CALIFORNIA PRESS**
*Berkeley   Los Angeles   London*

# SHOVELING
# FUEL FOR A
*Errant Economists,*

*Shameful Spenders,* # RUNAWAY TRAIN

*and a Plan to Stop Them All*

BRIAN CZECH

University of California Press
Berkeley and Los Angeles, California

University of California Press, Ltd.
London, England

© 2000 by
The Regents of the University of California

Library of Congress Cataloging-in-Publication Data
Czech, Brian, 1960–
    Shoveling fuel for a runaway train : errant economists,
shameful spenders, and a plan to stop them all /
Brian Czech.
      p. cm.
    Includes bibliographical references and index.
    ISBN 978-0-520-22514-5 (paper : alk. paper)
    1. Economic development—Economic aspects.
2. Consumption (Economics).   3. Neoclassical school of
economics.   4. Stagnation (Economics)   I. Title.
HD75.6.C97 2000
338.9—dc21

                          00-022311

Manufactured in the United States of America
15   14   13   12   11   10   09
10  9  8  7  6  5  4  3

Part One is dedicated to the Native American tribes, whose struggle for sustainability in the wake of a new American economy is a legitimate source of human pride.

Part Two is dedicated to the grandkids. May they inherit a democratic society, a sustainable economy, some wild country, and a generous dose of common sense. And may they have some fun in the process.

# CONTENTS

# ACKNOWLEDGMENTS

Because this book had no funding source, there are no financial contributors to acknowledge. However, I thank Paul Krausman for finding ways to keep me employed at the University of Arizona for an entire year following my doctoral program. Although my postdoctoral research had little to do with this book, the employment gave me the economic stability required to gather materials and begin writing. I also thank Paul—a fellow biologist and good friend—for encouraging me to study economic growth theory and for having the fortitude to co-author journal articles broaching the topic of economic growth.

I thank David King, Ed de Steiguer, John Gowdy, Richard Norgaard, Jack Isaacs, and the late Julie Leones, six economists who generously granted me their time to discuss the history of economic thought, economic growth theory, and a wide variety of economic concepts. I thank Eugene Maughan, Ed de Steiguer, and Christine Szuter for reviewing draft portions of the book, and Margo Martinez, Shirley Czech, Cecelia Gonzales, John Gowdy,

Richard Norgaard, Jeanne Clarke, and Deborah Green for reviewing early drafts of the entire manuscript. I thank Doris Kretschmer for her editorial ability, patience, and enthusiasm.

I especially thank Margo Martinez for her librarian expertise, willingness to serve as a theoretical sounding board, and unwavering encouragement.

# PROLOGUE
*A Wilderness Trail*
*to an Economic Tale*

The only parts of Jake above water were his lips and nostrils, gasping at the precious oxygen in the cold Nevada air. The north fork of the Humboldt River had the rest of him entombed in frigid, churning snowmelt. I was too cold to be frantic as I cut the diamond hitch from his left side, hoping the plastic milk crates I called panniers (which contained most of my life's possessions) would not rush away in the current. My campfire knife-sharpening diligence paid off as the buck knife sliced cleanly through the half-inch rope. On shore was the ranch hand Victor Bradfield, whom I had met in mutual shock minutes before by showing up at his door, dripping from head to foot with icy Humboldt water. I had explained my disastrous crossing—how I had swum with the horses from the south bank, got swept immediately downstream, barely grabbed a willow overhanging the north bank, and pulled myself desperately ashore—all less than 200 yards from Bradfield's line camp. Now Bradfield led my saddle horse Red steadily forward through the sleet. Jake the bay horse, lead rope dallied to Red's saddlehorn, was pulled from the grasp of premature death. When Jake finally made it to his feet, part of the waterlogged packload sagging off his right side, he stood shivering uncontrollably for a solid ten minutes before he could move to the shelter of a tack shed a quarter mile away.

This was but one hardship Red, Jake, and I faced during the early spring of 1983. The Great Basin had flooded, washing out Interstate 80 and generally wreaking havoc. The flood was of special interest to me, because I happened to be riding horseback from Benson, Arizona, to Kuna, Idaho. The flood and the weather leading up to it had already caused me problems, and were bound to cause more. Two weeks before, I'd found myself holed up for three days in a Ruby Valley blizzard, subsisting on venison jerky in the tent and periodically emerging to chop ice from a windmill trough for the horses. Two weeks after the Humboldt crossing, up on the Duck Valley Indian Reservation, I would have to ride along the highway, which was the only thing above water for miles around.

There were a lot of interesting things about that trip, flood or no flood, right from the start. There was an encounter with the San Pedro River on the second day out, when the tables were turned and Jake had to pull Red out of belly-deep quicksand. There was the morose and mysterious "security guard" threatening me with his pistol as I tried to water my horses at a supposedly abandoned gas station. There was wild Dave Erickson, who had moved his cattle operation to rough and dry Arizona, just so he could have wilder cattle to chase. There was old Joe Salvi, the 95-year-old Italian rancher entrenched in the shadow of Ruby Dome, complete with double hernia, toothless gums, roll-your-own smokes, and a 60-year-old indoor wooden swimming pool plumbed into a hot spring in his back yard. (Now *that* feller had some stories!)

The trip really was an adventure, which is why I took it to begin with, and friends kept telling me, "You ought to write a book about it." Well, fifteen years later, here I am writing a book, not quite about it, but about something I began to think about as I crossed the Sonoran, Mojave, and Great Basin deserts. I began to think about it because of periodic encounters with American mega-economy, some of which were very helpful. For instance, during frontier times, upon seeing the mighty Colorado River in my path, I might have turned around and gone back to Benson. But in 1983, there was Hoover Dam, the seventh wonder of the unnatural world. True, we had a mild wreck when Red spooked from the strangeness of it all and dumped me off on the hairpin turns leading down to the dam. But I learned my lesson, gathered up the horses, and led them to the Nevada side without feeling a drop of Colorado River.

I was no Jim Bridger. First of all, there were my own shortcomings with navigation and horsemanship. Of course, these I may have overcome at some point, to some extent. More importantly, though, there was no frontier! There were no grizzly bears and few mountain lions. Every time I thought I was getting into some wild country, an interstate highway and its high-tensile fences would block my path, the incredible candlepower of Phoenix would appear on the nighttime horizon, a jeep would come bouncing out of nowhere, a 200-foot-high powerline would transform the landscape, or a military jet would roar overhead. I thought a lot about these things, because they were always there to interrupt whatever peaceful thoughts I was having.

Don't get the wrong impression. You are not embarking on

some environmental radical's manifesto. After all, as soon as I got back to Idaho, I relinquished my firefighting position at the edge of the River of No Return Wilderness to take the thinning crew foreman position in town. The thinning crew is the motley outfit that goes into the forest with chainsaws and culls out trees so that the remaining trees grow faster and taller, which is good for timber production. And we didn't limit ourselves to the scruffy undergrowth, because our charge included "worthless tree removal." Subalpine fir or, as the loggers called it, "piss fir," was worthless on the timber market. Like most of the crew, I was a man in my early twenties and full of adrenaline, and I reveled in falling subalpine fir as broad at the stump as the hood of a small truck. I thought I knew what my Uncle Ben the logger must have felt like during the California heyday of the mid-1900s.

Like many of the loggers, thinners, and other folks I've known who worked in the woods, my mind wasn't totally devoid of academic thought. I professed to be, first and foremost, a wildlife biologist, complete with a bachelor's degree from the school where Aldo Leopold had created the profession in the 1930s. Trained about the habitat needs of other species, I knew that I was a living example of "competitive exclusion," the doctrine that one species can benefit only at the expense of some other. But I wasn't worried about it. My thinning activities and the logging that followed, by creating openings with large amounts of forage, were often beneficial to elk, at least, in the Idaho mountains. I thought I was participating in a win-win situation; the economy won and the elk (and hunters like me) won.

Then I spent a winter working construction in Dallas. The thirteen-story "hometel" that I helped build added to a ten-mile stretch of development leading west toward Arlington. When this stretch was included, seventy miles from the eastern outskirts of Dallas to the west edge of Fort Worth had been developed. At night I attempted (and occasionally succeeded at) maintaining a rental car building. I was working hard and playing hard, like most of the drifters on the construction site. But, living in a big city for the first time, I felt a bit disoriented. That was a bad feeling when crawling around on foot-wide ledges jutting out from the thirteenth floor, especially in the blustery winter winds with guys who seemed a little higher than the elevators took them.

I started getting cabin fever real bad, so I moved into an apartment on the outskirts of Arlington with a similarly misplaced high school buddy. I had quit the night job, having met my monetary goals for the winter. One evening I went out for a stroll. I found a newly constructed golf course, surrounded by newly developing subdivisions abutting our newly constructed apartment building. I was having a relatively enjoyable time of it, watching the nighthawks and poorwills come out and, believe it or not, a beaver! One they had obviously released in one of the fake ponds. It slapped the water with its tail and reminded me of then not-so-distant days in my native Wisconsin. That poor beaver was way out of place, but for a wildlifer, she was a sight for sore eyes.

On the way back in the darkness, I was in good spirits, thinking about beavers and real ponds and big rivers and the Idaho that awaited my return. Then suddenly the ground disappeared from beneath my feet. An instant later I found myself with one foot puckered on a horizontal piece of rebar, forearms straining on top of a newly installed manhole ring, eyes pondering in astonishment the newly uninstalled manhole cover sitting on the ground three feet away. But I came away with only a stress fracture in my right foot and escaped to Idaho a week later. As a working man who never made it to the opera, I never missed an inch of that seventy-mile stretch of noise.

I didn't stay in Idaho very long, though, because I got promoted to the position of wilderness ranger in the Teton Wilderness Area of Wyoming. I was stationed one mile south of the Yellowstone border, eight miles west of the Great Divide, and two days horseback from the nearest trailhead. This was big game paradise, and my favorite place of all time. Probably not for long, though—the Teton Wilderness is perilously close to the bustling touropolis of Jackson Hole.

From Wyoming, I went to work for the National Marine Fisheries Service on the Bering Sea. I had never been at sea, and— wouldn't you know—the worst storm of the winter hit during my first three days out. I was on a fifty-seven-meter Japanese stern trawler, and for three days it went "BAM . . . BAM . . . BAM" in ten-second intervals as thirty-foot waves crashed against the hull and swept over the decks. Periodically there was a "BAM . . . BAM . . . BA-BoiyoiyoiyoiyaaAAAAng" as the ship got way out of rhythm and got quartersided by a giant concave wall of water. No one could eat or sleep because of the constant, violent movement and booming noise, and even the Japanese who had spent years at sea were vomiting liberally. Worse yet, no one else spoke English, leaving only my imagination to interpret the structural impact of those unsettling hull reverberations.

But then the seas settled, we ate like hell, and fishing commenced. I'll never forget that first catch, the largest of the whole two-month stint. I logged it in at ninety-nine metric tons. We're talking hundreds of thousands of fish, almost all of which were pollock. I started to wonder how we could stay out very long, because surely the holds couldn't store many catches like this. Then

I saw how it worked. Male fish were summarily tossed to the floor, sloshed by the ship's movements into the bilge pumps and back out to sea as a sort of ichthyological hamburger. Females were treated the same, except that their egg sacs were taken prior to tossing. We had hit the peak of spawning, and while it lasted, supply and demand called for this type of wanton waste. This was my firsthand introduction to the "invisible hand" of the free market. I didn't think of it in those terms yet. I only termed it a hell of a lot of waste and damn sure wrong. But out of sight, out of mind, at least until days of retrospection.

During my report-writing and debriefing in Seattle, I had to ride a bus back and forth from the YMCA to National Marine Fisheries Service headquarters. This was a time of hard choices. I was twenty-six, and for the past ten years I hadn't lived in one place for more than nine months. Despite my travels and travails (or maybe because of them), no one was pounding on the door offering me a permanent biologist job. Most of the jobs were in federal government, and it was the heyday of veterans' preference and Equal Employment Opportunity, with Graham-Rudman budget cuts right around the corner. I was a healthy male who had missed the Vietnam draft by two years; my chances of federal employment were about as high as a pollock's in the Bering Sea. I was thinking seriously about moving on to a new field, when I noticed on the daily bus ride that I was going right past the University of Washington. On a whim, I pulled the string, asked for directions, and headed to the wildlife department. I talked to a few faculty members, each of whom pointed me toward Dr. Kenneth Raedeke, the large-mammal specialist and, as it turned out, a fun guy and a good friend. I found Ken and gave him my story. My story included some elk hunting tales from Idaho, and I promptly latched onto an elk study at Mt. St. Helens for my master's degree.

Now for non-wildlifers and aspiring wildlifers, it just doesn't happen that way, not normally. You normally compete to see if you can get accepted to work and study your tail off, pay thousands of dollars for the privilege, and get your degree. But I got to "work tail" and pay thousands with virtually no competition because the need for my services was immediate.

My elk research at Mt. St. Helens had to do with determining the impact of opening a road to tourists along the edge of the volcanic blast zone, which was then only six years old. So I darted and radio-collared elk, learned their habits, and documented the modifications in their behavior and habitat use after the road was opened. The elk study was fun and rather benign; the study area was only a temporary foraging grounds anyway because it would be heavily timbered in a few decades. The study was a lot more fun the first year, before they opened the gates to tens of thousands of tourists each month. Now Mt. St. Helens gets millions of visitors a year. Anyway, I gave them my recommendations pertaining to the use of the road, and I hear they used them to some extent.

But what really impressed me was the surrounding country and activities. Here were whole mountainsides stripped of timber, and not just in the blast zone! Mother Nature had done it to the blast zone; Boise Cascade and some other corporate giants had handled the rest. And all this in the midst of the Gifford Pinchot National Forest, named after the first professional forester in the United States. Pinchot was Theodore Roosevelt's right-hand man and the progenitor of the utilitarian conservation movement, which espoused the "greatest good for the greatest number of people, over the greatest period of time." What I saw on the private lands interspersed among the federal lands seemed more like the greatest cash flow for the smallest number over the shortest period. Not conservation, but liquidation. Even the Forest Service lands were heavily cut over, but it was harder to tell because at least the Forest Service left "sucker strips" to keep the clearcuts out of view from the roads. And, to be fair, the cuts were not as massive as those on the corporate lands.

Here I received my introduction to the spotted owl controversy. I went haywire over a young lady doing owl research, so I hung out with her and incidentally learned about owls. I also met some local folks who were downright dangerous in their adamancy against anything having to do with owls, if it meant slowing the flow of timber. In ecological terms, though, it was pretty obvious to a biologist what the problem was. The spotted owl was a species that nested in old-growth forest, which was being rapidly liquidated. Not only that, I didn't see how some of these areas would ever produce the *timber* they had in the past, what with whole exposed slopes sloughing off and messing up the rivers.

I think it was at this point when I started to think, little by little, in terms of economic growth. I had never pondered the economic significance of pollock roe, but I knew how important wood was to me, from pencils to packsaddles. And I had seen firsthand how important wood (along with all sorts of other raw materials) was to that vast acreage of development in the Dallas–Fort Worth area.

After my master's research, I went back to the Teton Wilderness to map grizzly bear habitat for the Forest Service. The highlight of that stint was the night my partner and I were camped on one ridge and one of the lighting strikes that started the Yellowstone fires of 1988 torched the next ridge to the east. We rode out the next day to behold a city of tents at the Blackrock Ranger Station. One of the most futile firefighting efforts in history had begun, and it ran on into early fall. But by some accounts it wasn't all bad. After all, it contributed tens of millions of dollars to our gross national product. Toward the end, I hired on to build a wildlife management program for the San Carlos Apache Tribe in Arizona.

The San Carlos Apache Reservation is the fourth largest Indian reservation in the country, and it's loaded with cowboy and Indian lore from the days when Generals Crook and Miles chased Geronimo around the Southwest. But from a wildlifer's perspective, it's a classic set of ecosystems, ranging from Sonoran Desert canyonlands in the south to Douglas fir forests in the north. Elk, mule deer, Coues whitetail, pronghorn antelope, desert bighorn sheep, Rocky Mountain bighorn, javelina, black bear, mountain lion, and wild turkey roam the reservation at will. Not only diversity, but quantity and quality abound. The largest elk antlers in the world come from San Carlos, and some of the highest densities of bears and lions in the United States benefit from the unruly cattle management. I could tell stories all day about the sights and sounds: walking in the moonlight amongst enormous, battling bull elk; waking up in the woods with a bear staring at me from three feet away; hunting deer only to discover a mountain lion hunting alongside. But you simply can't do these things justice on paper or, as the director of the San Carlos Cattle Association used to say, "under the artificial lights."

I was first drawn to the artificial lights when our top-notch Recreation and Wildlife director, Jim Higgs, was given the boot in a political coup. He had hired me and been the best boss I'd ever had. Higgs was a short man—short like a badger—and one of the most fearless men I've met. An ex-Arizona Game and Fish ranger, he was a better shot than any of the game rangers at San Carlos, which was mighty good. He was a wily character in wild country, naturally and politically. Surviving one political crisis after another for four years, Higgs did miracles for the Recreation and Wildlife Department until he was unceremoniously dropped like a hot rock. I was afraid of what could happen to the department if the leading contender (a political schemer who didn't know a black bear from a prickly pear) got the director position. Besides, I remembered the words of Orin Rongstad, who provided our department orientation at University of Wisconsin-Madison ten years earlier: "If you really want to do something for wildlife, get out of here and go into politics!"

After three months of political turmoil, I took over as director and promptly deposited heart and soul into department affairs. Our annual revenue went from $800,000 to $1.2 million, our budget from $500,000 to $870,000. But there was a minefield of toes to get through, including some I couldn't avoid. After two more years of political turmoil, I met the same fate as ol' Higgs. Which was fine with me. I'd done my job and it was time to move on. As one of the tribal Game and Fish commissioners had said at the time of my appointment, "If you don't get fired, you're not doing your job." And I'd learned a valuable lesson; Orin Rongstad was right. A little political effort went a long way in the field; we had completed all kinds of habitat improvement projects with our newly acquired capital.

But there was a certain irony to these efforts. The reservation was big game country for two main reasons. First of all, it had the prerequisite natural endowment. Second, it lacked the well-developed economy that had usurped so many hunting grounds off-reservation. While I displayed our profits as proof positive that wildlife was more important to the tribal economy than the struggling cattle operations or the subsidized timber program, might those same profits gradually threaten their own existence? The thought couldn't escape me during my last year at San Carlos, when I negotiated the sale of three special elk tags for $43,000 each, the highest-priced elk tags in the nation that year. Two of them I sold to the owner of the largest old-growth sawmill in the Northwest, who flew in on his own Lear jet; the other went to an investment banker from the Northeast. The money went to a good cause (the Dry Lake Elk Habitat Improvement Fund), but where did the money come from? What were we really promoting? Were the net economics beneficial in a broad sense? You be the judge, but preferably after you've read the book.

When I left the tribe, I got accepted at the University of Arizona for a doctoral program in renewable natural resources studies. Now I was pretty much committed to the artificial lights. I wanted to broaden my horizons, get some formal policy training, and head back into the work force at a national level with greater political and professional license. I conducted a policy analysis of the Endangered Species Act for my dissertation, applying a new model called policy design theory, which was developed by one of my committee members, the eminent political scientist Helen Ingram.

But something happened before I could get back into the work force. I got a little sidetracked. Policy design theory turned out to be one of the most comprehensive forms of policy analysis devised. It took the best and brightest contributions from political science and compacted them into a grand schematic that questioned policy to its core, and prescribed serving democracy above all else. By comprehensive I mean, for example, that my analysis of the Endangered Species Act had to encompass not only the logical, technical, and political aspects of the act itself, but the socioeconomic context in which the act was embedded (and still is). And what a revelation *that* was. By the time I was done, I concluded that if I ever stood in Rongstad's boots, I would repeat what he said, but with a slight twist: "If you really want to do something for wildlife, democracy, or the grandkids, go into political economy." And so my days in the wild came to an end, and here I sit under the artificial lights, writing a book on political economy for the sake of the grandkids.

PART ONE

# THE RUNAWAY TRAIN

The great truisms of economics have no clear discoverers; they are evident for all to see.

JOHN KENNETH GALBRAITH,
*Economics in Perspective*, 1987

When you have eliminated the impossible, whatever remains, however improbable, must be the truth.

SIR ARTHUR CONAN DOYLE,
*The Sign of Four*, 1889

# ECONOMIC GROWTH
# AS A NATIONAL GOAL

"We should *double* the rate of growth, and we should *double* the size of the American economy!" hailed candidate Jack Kemp during the vice presidential debate of October 9, 1996. Kemp was firing away from the bandwagon, and there's never been a redder face under whiter hair. He knew Americans have long been instilled with the ideal that economic growth is good, that economic growth solves societal problems. He figured they would vote for the candidate who could pull off the most growth. Less emphatic, Kemp's opponent Al Gore nevertheless sanctioned the growth race with the impeccably wry retort, "Well, the economy is growing very strongly right now. . . . The average growth rate is also coming up. It is higher than in either of the last two *Republican* administrations."

At face value, the argument that economic growth is good is hard to deny. After all, the economic growth of a nation is taken to mean that its citizens will be better fed, dressed, housed, educated, transported, and entertained. More MacDonald's and Antoine's, more Fords and Fiats, more jeep trails and ship sails. For rich and for poor, more quantity of more things. *Twice* as much, if we elect Jack Kemp. So economic growth leads to a better life, at least a better material life. This argument will be left intact for the time being. I mention it here only to explain the esteemed status of economic growth in the American psyche.

How esteemed is the status? At the University of Arizona, I conducted a nationwide survey and simply asked people. I presented them with a series of concepts, and found that economic growth is valued at a level of 75.4 on an importance scale of zero to 100, putting it in the same category as property rights and species conservation (Czech and Krausman 1999). Democracy and ecosystem health were valued at an even higher level, but none of these were valued as highly as the availability of resources for posterity (at 85.8). So Americans value economic growth quite highly, but perhaps not insanely so.

Another method with which to estimate esteem is to look at the news surrounding economic growth. Surely the newspapers wield a great influence on, and are affected by, the American attitude toward economic growth. I tapped into the National Newspaper Index, which catalogs articles from such bellwether papers as the *New York Times, Washington Post, Wall Street Journal*, and *Los Angeles Times*. From them are spawned many of the syndicated, copied, or emulated columns that grace the smaller rags throughout the nation. I searched for the phrase "economic growth" and found reference to 1,930 articles. In the uniform sample of every twentieth article I examined, economic growth was *always* treated as a desirable phenomenon. In nearly 15 percent of the articles, though the *rate* of growth for this or that region was considered too high, the propriety of growth itself was never questioned. No wonder Americans have such a positive view of economic growth!

One especially attention-grabbing article was "Stupid students, smart economy?" in which Robert J. Samuelson (1998) entertained an argument that despite the education crisis perceived by many Americans, we shouldn't worry. In this view, the fact that economic growth continues is a sure sign of an intelligent, well-educated society. Imagine the sighs of relief such a proposal must have produced amidst the angst over American schools. But does a perpetual increase in American consumption of goods and services really mean that its citizens are smarter? Has there ever been a bigger dog wagged by a smaller tail?

Then there is the evening news. Trends on Wall Street reflect the growth of the economy, and on each of the major broadcasting networks a stock market report is provided day in and day out. Gains on Wall Street are invariably presented as good news, while losses are decried, although perspective is sometimes evident to the extent that losses are termed "corrections." "Leading economic indicators" are also closely monitored. Housing starts, net corporate profits, and disposable income motivate Wall Street reaction. Again, upward trends are invariably portrayed as good. No other TV news topic receives daily monitoring at the national scale, suggesting that American society has no greater obsession than with economic growth—aforementioned survey results notwithstanding.

In addition to our political leaders and news media, our bureaucracy upholds economic growth as a national goal. On the first page of her annual report for fiscal year 1992, Barbara Hackman Franklin (Republican Secretary of Commerce) said, "Rec-

ognizing that commerce has supplanted military and security issues as the main concerns among nations, the 14 diverse agencies
that make up the Commerce Department rallied . . . to advance
a seven point agenda for fostering economic growth." Not to be
outdone, in his annual report for fiscal year 1994, the late Ronald
Brown (Democratic Secretary of Commerce) said, "The activities of the Department— promoting economic growth through
[a myriad of techniques]—have worked in strategic harmony to
provide increased economic security for all Americans." The primary, perennial, and bipartisan goal of this massive, cabinet-level
department is economic growth.

Even government agencies that are supposed to play an ac-
tive role in conservation pursue the mission of economic growth.
The Army Corps of Engineers, for example, is the oldest natural resource agency in the federal government and responsible
for much of the nation's water quality and wetlands conservation. Since the 1970s, the Army Corps has defined its mission
in terms of four programs: national economic development, regional economic development, environmental quality, and social
well-being. In 1983, consistent with President Ronald Reagan's
emphasis on regulatory impact assessment, the Corps formally
prioritized economic development.

Reflecting on trends in American economic policy since his
stint as an economic advisor to President Richard Nixon, Herbert
Stein lamented, "Growth is now the great god before whom all
participants in the discussion of economic policy bow their knee.
Merely to allege that a policy will promote growth is sufficient to
make a case for it" (from Hamrin 1988:40).

In addition to public esteem and official sanction, economic
growth is the subject of much American faith. It is a particularly

American feature that each generation believes the following one should and will attain a higher economic standard of living. A 1994 survey found that 63 percent of Americans agreed that there were *no* limits to economic growth (Madrick 1995). Even our Secretary of the Interior, Bruce Babbitt, after delivering a litany of species endangered by economic development, announced, "But there is no conflict between wildlife conservation and economic development. We can grow without limit." (I have no citation for Babbitt's statement, but I was there in March of 1997 when it was delivered at the 62nd North American Wildlife and Natural Resources Conference in Washington, D.C. I copied it into my notes, discussed it briefly with an overscheduled Babbitt afterward, and brought it up in the open forum later that day. The director of the U.S. Fish and Wildlife Service, Jamie Clark, got stuck dealing with it.)

Understandably, American citizens can hardly resist the continually reinforcing influence of their news media, bipartisan politicians, and government. Or vice versa. But as one studies the phenomenon of economic growth as national ideal, one discovers that all the politicians, news reporters, and bureaucrats combined have only been following the lead of a privileged class of experts. After all, who wrote the syndicated column? Who did the reporter interview on the evening news? Who taught the politician, the bureaucrat, and the citizen what they know about economics? Why the economists, of course.

Economics is a topic that most of us avoid due to its dry, mathematically tedious bearing. My introductory macroeconomics course at the University of Wisconsin had the highest proportion of sleepers of any class I've seen. Most of us bought class notes and just skipped the damned thing. The only thing that lifted the tedium was when a pigeon would get into the towering chamber of Bascom Hall, or when Professor Culbertson would flail away at an intrusive bumblebee. Leave it to Mother Nature to breathe some semblance of life into economics.

We nevertheless live in a society shaped by economists. Malthus, Mill, and Marx established the great debates of Western civilization in the 1800s. They and their cohorts attained the ponderous status of "classical economists," partly in reference to their place in academic time. Thomas Malthus in 1805, for instance, became the first professor of political economy in the English-speaking world. Not coincidentally, it was also a time when a new, capitalistic society offered a way out of the dark ages of feudalistic warmongering, callous kings and queens, and bartering one's way to relative comfort. But "classical" best befits the fact that these economists were much more than number crunchers. The Adam Smiths and the David Ricardos spoke of big, classic issues like the power of nations, the distribution of wealth, and the limits of land. They were political philosophers and beacons of light in a truly new world order. As a group, they produced some of the most influential books ever written, including *Wealth of Nations* (Smith), *An Essay on the Principle of Population* (Malthus), and *Principles of Political Economy* (Ricardo).

The field of economics, then, rests on a fabulous foundation of human thought. But something went awry in twentieth-century western economics. For one thing, it dropped the big issues. As Robert Heilbroner (1992 : 173) put it, "economics had ceased to be the proliferation of world views that, in the hands of now a philosopher [Smith], now a stockbroker [Ricardo], now a revolutionary [Marx], seemed to illuminate the whole avenue down which society was marching. It became instead the special province of professors, whose investigations threw out pinpoint beams rather than the wide-searching beacons of the earlier economists." This new brand of economics gradually distilled the classicists' efforts into a unified assumption that economic growth is good, pure and simple. So today in a typical introductory textbook (Ekelund and Tollison 1988:147), students read that "The overall goal of macroeconomic policy is the achievement of economic stabilization . . . to attain maximum economic growth in the present and future." Economics thus became a science geared toward justifying and facilitating the pursuit of wealth by individuals and nations. In perhaps its most radical departure from the classicists, however, it adopted the assumption that there is no limit to economic growth. In the process, it misinterpreted Smith, denied Malthus and Mill, and ignored Marx. This twentieth-century school of thought came to be known as "neoclassical" (new and different) economics, and it is the mainstream economics today.

When the word "economics" is used without any qualifying adjectives by a reporter, politician, or bureaucrat, it invariably means neoclassical economics. When someone speaks of an alternative school of economic thought, like "ecological economics" (which will be explained later), an adjective is used. But unless your reading interests take you deeply into the sphere of economics, the economics you encounter will almost certainly be neoclassical. Of course, as with most highly developed fields of study, there are alternative views of how the economics discipline may be classified. In one alternative, neoclassical economics was born with the tenure of Alfred Marshall at Cambridge in the late 1800s. In another, neoclassical economics is simply an elaboration of classical economics, both passing away around 1959 with the death of Arthur Pigou (chair of political economy at Cambridge

from 1908 to 1944). In this view, the current predominant model
is classified as Keynesian economics (a classification to be partly
explained in the following paragraph and further in chapter 2).
But most economics texts and practitioners employ the "neoclassical synthesis," classifying Keynesian economics as a special
case of neoclassical theory, and that is the convention I will follow. All this may sound a bit confusing, but the important point
is that neoclassical economics, in this book and in most others,
refers to the collective body of economic theory that dominates
economics today.

Riding on the shoulders of the classical giants, the neoclassical economists' expertise has long been sought by politicians and
high-level bureaucrats who want to know what actions to take
to better the lot of humankind—not to mention obtaining more
votes and bigger salaries. It all started when John Maynard
Keynes, Marshall's star pupil and champion of macroeconomic
manipulation, helped the western world to think it was figuring
its way out of the Great Depression. But the thought that subsequent neoclassical economists could be wrong about the limits to
economic growth has not received serious attention anywhere in
mainstream society. Certain radical economists and many ecologists have objected, but their arguments are seldom heard outside
of academia. That is partly because science is too dry for most
Americans. After all, if you work forty hours a week and take care
of a family, you don't want to read about dull serious stuff in your
spare time. Also, people in academia (university professors, primarily) tend to be competitive and egotistical. You have to be
competitive to make a living in academia, and competitiveness
is a natural counterpart to egotism. Just like football players want
to be known for gaining the most yards or scoring the most

points, professors want to be known for having the most profound thoughts or publishing the most scientific journal articles.

Note that I did not say publishing the most books or newspaper articles. Professors in the sciences (as opposed to those in the arts) differ from football players in that they generally care little about what the "fans" think. The ones they need to impress, if not for their own egos then for their professional advancement in the university system, are other scientists. And the currency that scientists deal in is scientific journal articles, in which scientists compete to display academic originality. Because all the simple things have been said in many ways, demonstrating a pioneering thought is difficult to do without writing something incredibly complex. So, for instance, Professor Bhaskar (1981 : 363) writes, "scientific development involves a fallible dialectic of explanatory and taxonomic knowledge, on which modified Aristotelian and Lockean realist positions in the theory of universals and perception respectively are seen to be entailed." Meanwhile, Professor Hannon and his colleagues (1986 : 397) write, "A sufficient condition for the equality of energy intensities calculated using the commodity-technology assumption (Eq. (8)) and the process-technology assumption (Eq. (10)) is that the commodity weightings in the process-technology assumption are the energy intensities, i.e., $p = \varepsilon$." (In case you're wondering, Eq. 8 was $\varepsilon(c,c) = E^P g^{-1} C^{-1} (I - BC^{-1})^{-1}$ and Eq. 10 was . . . , ah forget it.)

This is not to say that professors from the sciences never write for the general public. But few do regularly, and even fewer do successfully. In the sciences, you are trained *not* to write in an entertaining fashion that would be enjoyed by the general public. Science is dry stuff, and rightfully so. Dry language guards against the tainting of scientific findings by emotion, trickery, and inefficiency. Thus and thankfully, Professor Bhaskar did not write, "Believe it or not, scientific development involves a pathetic dialogue of redundant taxonomic knowledge, on which good-ol'-boy 'realist' positions in the freakishly contorted theories of perception are found to pile like a lot of crap!" After years of writing for science journals, writing with some semblance of style, grace, or humor becomes a real challenge (note the preceding) that few scientists invest time in, especially when academic competition calls for continual scientific writing. But occasionally one encounters a professor who seems to care less about what other professors think than what the public thinks, and puts forth the effort. Outstanding examples from economics include Robert L. Heilbroner and John Kenneth Galbraith.

In summary, economic growth is a cherished American ideal. It is touted by politicians of both parties, praised in newsprint, and monitored nightly on TV. It has long been a goal of our federal government, and supposedly has "surpassed military and security issues" as the prime federal concern. Trying to decide who is the driving force in this complicity of media, government, and citizens is a chicken/egg quandary. But aside from their historical value, chicken/egg arguments are always moot; once you have either, the other will follow. Even if the public were not enthralled with economic growth, surely it would become so given the continual psychological reinforcement of media and government minions. However, just as the chicken/egg argument overlooks the rooster, attributing America's obsession with economic growth to the public, government, or media overlooks the planter of the seed: the neoclassical growth economist.

# WHAT DID JACK KEMP REALLY SAY?

2

In his debate with Al Gore, Jack Kemp did not hail, "We should *double* the amount of materials we consume, and we should *double* the amount of waste we produce!" He knew that Americans have become concerned about conservation and especially about pollution. And he knew that Al Gore, who has some expertise in these matters, would have taken him severely to task. And yet, that's just about what Jack Kemp *did* say! Economic growth is an increase in the production and consumption of goods and services. To double the size of the petroleum sector (strictly defined and not including associated services) means to burn roughly twice as much oil. To double the size of the lumber economy means to produce roughly twice as much lumber, and to double the size of the fishing economy means to catch roughly twice as many fish.

How can we do any of these things? We've already resorted to pumping the Arctic slope of Alaska for oil, to save us from the mercy (or lack thereof) of the OPEC nations. The spotted owl controversy hints that a major lumber region has been producing above its capacity. Depleted fish stocks, including salmon in the Northwest and cod in the Northeast, say the same for fish. The principles are quite simple. You can't keep producing and consuming anything—goods or services—in perpetually increasing amounts, because (1) there are only so many raw materials available; (2) the raw materials are only replenished by nature at a certain rate, and some not at all; (3) there is only so much room in which to conduct economic activities; and (4) there is only so much space in which to store the waste products of economic activity.

Neoclassical economists have always figured out ways to skirt these hard realities. First, like some of their classical predecessors, they just ignored the issue and got away with it because resources were abundant in much of the world until fairly recently. Sure, Thomas Malthus had declared the mathematical certainty of populations outstripping their food supply, and David Ricardo had incorporated a similar assumption in his model of the economy. John Stuart Mill had spoken in sweeping terms about the limits to economic expansion (to be explored in chapter 5). Even Adam Smith and his colleague David Hume had seen, way out on the horizon, an end to the accumulation process. But these classical visions, which were scarcely relevant at the time, lost most of the relevancy they had as soon as agriculture took a back seat to the Industrial Revolution. Furthermore, once the age of colonialism arrived, there was always another country that could be colonized or emigrated to. The biggest and best example was the United States with its abundance of wood, water, grass, coal, minerals, wildlife, and other natural resources. The plenitude of the land was so awe-inspiring that the thought of limits was, quite understandably, the farthest thing from the minds of most nineteenth-century economists.

To put ourselves in similar shoes, we might try to think about what to do when the sun runs out of hydrogen, like the astronomers tell us will happen in a few billion years. It can't hold our attention very long, because it is a premature topic. To a lesser degree but along the same lines, so was it premature in the nineteenth century to worry about limits to economic growth. Especially in the United States where timber stood tall, prairies stretched from horizon to horizon, and fish clogged the rivers from sea to shining sea, economists concerned themselves with issues of value, price, and the distribution of wealth.

Even when regional resource shortages made their ominous American appearance at the dawn of the twentieth century, the recently christened neoclassical economists continued to ignore the limits to growth, and again got away with it because there were needs that seemed more pressing on the surface. There were the waves of European immigrants and the economic upheaval they brought, so distributional issues remained at the fore. There were the mighty and menacing monopolies, too, so trust-busting got special attention. Eventually there was the Great Depression and its devastating unemployment. Which brings us back to Keynes.

John Maynard Keynes himself was born into wealth and prestige, and spent much of his life hobnobbing with top-level politicians, meritorious scholars, and cultural trendsetters in his native England. When he didn't start out at the top, he went straight there, like when he wrote a letter to President Franklin Roosevelt and had it published in the *New York Times* on the closing day of 1933. The letter exhorted Roosevelt to spend federal money on public works, thus stimulating production and consumption in the private sector, even though such a policy would put the federal treasury into debt. This was a revolutionary departure from the noninterventionist policies inherited from classical times, where Adam Smith's invisible hand would paternally allocate resources and distribute wealth, and where "Say's law" would ensure the employment of all. Roosevelt did precisely what Keynes recommended, too—in fact, he had already started spending federal money on public-works projects, out of political necessity. Even without Keynes or Depression politics, such massive public investment would have eventually been necessitated by World War II. But Keynes's high profile, and perhaps Roosevelt's potential need for a scapegoat, made it appear that Keynes and his colleagues were the guiding light of the New Deal.

Keynes's encore wasn't bad, either. His 1936 book, *The General Theory of Employment, Interest and Money*, served to detail his thoughts on stimulating economies via government intervention. Although it was scarcely readable by anyone but economists, economists had become quite influential, and Keynes's book became one of the most influential of all time.

Keynes gave economics a heavy hand in government, with a proverbial slap on the invisible wrist. But not all economists chose to enter into public debate. Many, if not most, preferred to keep clear of policy issues in order to keep the science of economics free of secularism. In a way, they are more important to the topic of this book, because they avoided addressing immediate problems like the Depression. Even though these economic scholars were told of resource shortages in the real world, they felt free to develop a set of theoretical concepts consistent with the model of perpetual economic growth.

The first such concept was substitutability, which said that the factors of economic production (land, labor, and capital) could be substituted among themselves. For example, if land became scarce, more production could be squeezed from it if only more labor was applied, or more capital utilized, or both. The substitutability concept was extended to assert that a resource could not be depleted, because as it was extracted and the pickings got slim, another resource could be substituted for it. For example, when coal becomes scarce and its price gets high, we turn to oil. When oil becomes scarce, we turn to gas. When gas becomes scarce, take your pick from nuclear, hydro, solar, or even cow power. This is a very simple concept, and it doesn't take an economist to make it obvious. However, common sense also suggests that, at some point, substitution might not keep up with the demands of a growing economy.

Take lumber, for instance. White pine boards from the northern Great Lakes fed the appetite for the burgeoning laissez faire economy, until the great pine forests were used up toward the end of the nineteenth century. The remaining slash piles and scrubby second-growth forests went up in balls of flame, as in Wisconsin's devastating Peshtigo fire of 1871, and the boom towns dropped off the map. So the lumber industry, looking for a white pine substitute, turned to the deep South. The great bald cypress swamps were drained, and pullboat logging proceeded to liquidate the bald cypress by the 1920s. The boom towns died and the lumber industry turned to California. The redwoods went down, and it was on to the Northwest with its western redcedar, Douglas fir, and Sitka spruce.

I witnessed part of the next phase, which also has largely passed. The days on the Gifford Pinchot National Forest when you had to thread your way on narrow mountain roads, past logging trucks loaded to full capacity with a single log, have already been substituted for by the days when environmentalists spike trees and loggers punch noses. Now we get some boards from the Southeast with its loblolly, slash, and shortleaf pine, but these species are mostly geared to pulp and paper production. So now we consume 30 percent more lumber, and 13 percent more wood in general, than we produce (Brownridge 1990). We have become a nation of lumber importers. Now that's substitutability!

Of course, there is no way to thoroughly deny the neoclassical economist exclusively on the grounds of substitutability. After all, lumber can be and is substituted for—we framed plenty a room in that Dallas hometel with aluminum studs. Iron girders substituted for wood beams, and sheetrock for panelling. So by simply replacing the forests in your mind's eye with iron mines, you can observe the progression of mines and mining from the New England colonies to the western shores of Lake Superior, and again, all the way to our overseas suppliers, which is where most of our iron comes from now, too. Of course, when the costs of importing lumber and iron get high enough, we can log higher on our own slopes, dig deeper into our own continent, or turn to another substitute. Maybe plastic will get us by.

So, in a strict sense, the neoclassical economists are right. Due to the phenomenon of substitutability, resources do not become entirely depleted. But the key word is "entirely." As anyone who visits northern Wisconsin or southern Louisiana can attest, there is precious little white pine or bald cypress left, certainly no economically significant supply. And there won't be in a time frame short of geological, and perhaps never, because these fabulously forested landscapes have been ecologically transformed into runty popple woods and mucky truck farms, respectively. California has subdivision upon subdivision and Washington state has its sucker strips (those thin stands of unlogged forest along the roads). Ironically, substitutability as an economics concept is a poor substitute for the meaning of substitutability in the vernacular.

But that is not the only problem with the concept of substitutability. Other sectors of the economy are not so amenable to the application of the concept. Take any sector with a major dependence on fresh water, for instance. Right away, we can forget about finding an analogy to the construction sector's substituting of iron for wood, or plastic for iron. Water is water: two atoms of hydrogen, bonded with God's loving care to an atom of oxygen. That's all there is and there ain't no more. With water, the only way to apply the principle of substitutability is to substitute one water *source* for another. As we saw with lumber, this type of substitutability indeed has limits.

Due to the size of our population and its dependence on water for virtually everything it attempts, water supplies are degraded in every state in the country. Cornell University's David Pimentel and colleagues (1994:353) have warned that "The greatest threat to maintaining fresh water supplies is overdraft of surface and groundwater resources to supply the needs of the rapidly growing human population and of the agriculture which provides its food." They were not far from saying, "The greatest threat to maintaining economic growth is overdraft of water. . . . " Economic growth, remember, is the production and consumption of goods and services, and is a function of population size and per capita consumption. People require water to live. So to get more economic growth via population increase requires more people and therefore more water usage. To get more economic growth via per capita consumption requires more consumption by each person, and it is difficult to think of a single good or service that does not entail the consumption of water at some point in the process.

Groundwater supplies are in jeopardy throughout large portions of the United States. For example, water is drawn from the Oglala aquifer (underlying most of the southern Great Plains) at a rate 130 to 150 percent above its replacement rate, a rate that will allow production to increase for only about thirty-five more years. The mighty Colorado River trickles near its mouth like a midwestern creek, its waters spent by the populations of Colorado, Utah, Nevada, California, and Arizona. Seattle, of all places, spent the early 1990s in the news due to its water shortages and rationing program. Federal court reports are loaded with water cases from the West, illustrating the complex litigation and rulemaking demanded by economic growth.

In the eastern United States, pollution is the biggest threat to the water supply. The East is where rivers used to catch fire. Again, more rule-making was a byproduct of economic growth; the Lake Erie fishery almost died before the National Environmental Policy Act and the Clean Water Act came to the rescue. Even for those who dislike the federal government and its regulatory ways, did not the Environmental Protection Agency and Army Corps of Engineers do an admirable job? However, good policy-making and implementation can only treat symptoms for so long, and while Seattle was getting over the drought, Milwaukee water was in the news for killing consumers. Pollution is a function of human municipality and industry, which produces waste in direct proportion to the number of customers and their per capita consumption.

Some water supplies appear to be doing well until analyzed in an ecosystem context. For example, municipal water supplies in Florida have grown along with demand, but only via draining most of the Everglades. Now the Everglades are home to numerous endangered species, and are prone to drastic flooding during hurricanes because the sponging capacity of the Everglades has been lost.

Of course, we can expect neoclassical economists to argue that we have not begun to tap the waters of water substitutability. They may agree that water substitutability applies only to sources but can say that "sources" need not be limited to the vernacular. Instead of looking to a more distant aquifer or river, for example, we should be thinking about technologies like saltwater conversion, condensation plants, or the toting of icebergs from the Arctic to California. We can reply that these labor- and capital-intensive operations consume their own resources and cause their own pollution, but they will reply that once we get the right technology developed, the problem will be solved. Despite the ludicrousness with which we view such "solutions," we can't really win the argument. Not in theory, because until we *prove* that these solutions are untenable, the theory stands. That is how science proceeds. A theory stands until disproven.

We might protest by pointing out that, even if we were to truly tap all sources, from aquifers to icebergs to atmospheres, Earth and its atmosphere contain only so much hydrogen and oxygen. Then the neoclassical economists are expected to say, "But that's not a practical argument." Whereupon we could respond, "True, but in theory, it stands." We would have a valid and profound point, because once it is demonstrated that there is indeed a limit to economic growth, regardless of how far off that limit may seem, it provides an entirely different perspective from which the economists must view the world. They can argue that there is a great deal of economic growth that remains possible, but cannot argue strictly that economic growth may continue into infinity. And once the existence of a limit is established in theory, then perhaps the growth economists' emphasis will shift from finding more ingenious growth mechanisms to ascertaining how close we are to the limit.

There is one last weakness of the substitutability concept. Although it is theoretically powerful in its portrayal of economic production, it ignores the space available thereto. With the construction sector, where the substitutability concept is seen to work in a strict (if not in a vernacular) sense, one would ultimately come to the question of where to build an additional house or saltwater conversion plant or condensation facility. Neoclassical economists might answer, "Ultimately, in outer space." To which we might respond, "But that's not a practical argument." Whereupon they could say, "True, but in theory, it stands." They win again! (In theory).

Even before resorting to the "ultimate answer" of outer space, neoclassical economists can, to some extent, answer the spatial problem with the second concept employed to tout the infinitude of economic growth: efficiency. Economists use the term "efficiency" in several ways. In one sense, efficiency refers to the allocation of resources such that an *optimal* combination of outputs results. This allocative efficiency or optimization has long been a concern of welfare economics. The focus of economic growth theory, on the other hand, is on productive efficiency or productivity. Productivity is the output per unit of input employed, and increases in productivity are defined as resulting "from increased efficiency on the part of capital or labour" (Pearce 1992 : 348).

Increasing efficiency, in other words, allows the production of more goods and services with less land, labor, and capital. Efficiency is generally obtained via specialization of the production process, division of labor, and technological progress. So, for instance, as diesel engines become more efficient, less diesel fuel is required to dig more ditches, drain more wetlands, till more soil, plant and harvest more crops, and transport more grain. As factory work becomes more routinized, and factory equipment more streamlined, more gadgets come off the assembly line with less raw material and labor. On and on throughout all economic sectors. Again the principle is born of common sense, again the possibilities are endless in theory, again the theory seems too good to be true and probably is, but again disproof is a daunting task. Daunting but definitely worth discussing.

Efficiency is not a phenomenon monopolized by economics. Athletics is a revealing example of efficiency in action. Since records have been kept, athletes have continued to run faster, jump higher, and throw farther. The records mount as athletes use more efficient equipment, train more efficiently, and more efficiently nourish their bodies. Periodically a more efficient breakthrough method is discovered, as when high jumpers abandoned the relatively elaborate back flop for the more efficient frontal assault. Yet can we expect a high jumper to *double* the current world record, ever? And records are not the rule, but the exception. Shall we expect the average jumper of tomorrow to jump *twice* as high as the average jumper of today? Maybe, just maybe, if we think in terms of geological time, when our species becomes something quite different from the one our grammas and grampas belonged to. But we don't and we can't manage or plan anything, from a track meet to a national economy, in a geological time frame. We have to think in terms of years, decades, and, if we are concerned for posterity, centuries. Beyond that, we place our faith in untested theory at the great-grandkids' risk. And note, we haven't even had the audacity to ask whether the high jumper will be able to jump *ten* times as high, or a *hundred* times as high. Or *perpetually higher!*

For me, the athletic analogy comes to mind because an economist once described neoclassical growth theory in a nutshell as, "There may be a limit to growth at any one point in time, but the bar keeps inching upward. So over time, there really is no limit." Yet the continual athletic record-breaking we see in the managerial time frame is largely a function of increasingly accurate measurement, where the records get broken by diminishing margins. Early pole-vaulting records may have been broken by the inch; today they are broken by the hundredth of an inch. Tomorrow they will be broken by the thousandth, hardly a compelling argument for infinite progress. Ultimately, efficiency is limited by particle physics—no more raising the bar—but long before we get there the practical limit is reached. Such is the nature of efficiency in all of its manifestations, be they athletic, prosthetic, or economic. And neoclassical economists ought to be the experts on this! Their classical forebears did more than anyone in history to refine the concept of diminishing marginal returns.

Admittedly, economies are far more complex than athletics. We can look back in history and find truly revolutionary increases in economic efficiency. Again the lumber industry is a good example.

Allowing for a slight digression, in evolutionary theory it was once popular to surmise that "ontogeny recapitulates phylogeny," meaning that the development of an animal's body resembles the evolution of its species, to some extent at least. As a biologist I get a kick out of the saying, so I try to get it into circulation. Well, my forestry ontogeny recapitulates the timber industry phylogeny, to some extent at least. When I was a Youth Conservation Corps laborer in Wisconsin, our crew was too young and maybe too crazy to be trusted with power tools. So we cleared those diseased elm trees with big, long, two-man crosscut saws, just like they did in the 1800s when the loggers called them "misery whips." And the misery whip, even though it took two people to operate, was more than doubly efficient as two guys hacking away with one-man crosscut saws. A few years later in the Boise National Forest, where I assaulted the piss fir with my Model 048 Stihl, I discovered the miraculous efficiency of the chainsaw. But that was nothing. In Washington I watched them log with gigantic whole-tree harvesters that sever the log from the ground with one hydraulic squeeze, the logs brought to the yard via torque-happy helicopter. That pretty well summarizes the evolution of efficiency in the lumber industry, or at least in the logging portion thereof.

As for the sawing of logs, we saw what efficiency did in the Northwest. The mills were marvelously efficient at processing old-growth timber. So efficient, in fact, that most of the old mill workers were being laid off long before the old growth was gone. So efficient that the operators balked at re-tooling for second-growth, smaller timber, leading to the shutdown of the industry throughout much of the region.

Right away some problems in assessing efficiency appear. First of all, is whole-tree logging really more efficient? After all, when toiling with the misery whip, not a single ounce of petrol is consumed. A little bit is consumed with the chainsaw, and a great deal more with the whole-tree harvester. According to the neoclassical economist, the higher profit margin of whole-tree logging, where employed, is evidence for greater efficiency. But there are radical economists (of an ilk I shall describe in chapter 5) who point out that petroleum consumption trumps efficiency in its long-term implications for economic growth, because petroleum is a nonrenewable resource for all practical purposes. (Faced with limited petroleum supplies, the neoclassical economist may resort to substitutability arguments, with which we have already dealt, and to which we shall return.)

Furthermore, at least in the traditional model, the factors of economic production are land, labor, and capital, where "land" is understood to mean acreage and the natural resources thereon. The whole-tree harvester uses a tiny bit of labor, a unit of land (petroleum), and a very expensive unit of capital to sever the log. Not only expensive but very large—the road to a bigger economy is strewn with metallic hunks of yesterday's efficiency. Meanwhile, the misery whip operator uses a lot of labor and a cheap unit of capital that takes up precious little storage space. Whole-tree harvesting and helicopter logging may be more efficient for the men, whose labor consists of pushing levers in harvesters or pulling joysticks in helicopters. But what about the *net* energy efficiency, accounting for the petroleum (a unit of land) used? And, thence, what about for economic efficiency in the long term?

Clearly I chose this example to make the point that efficiency should not be taken at face value. But I would be building a strawman if I claimed that neoclassical economists base their assessments on face value. To the contrary, they have produced some incredibly elaborate assessments. The point, however, is that efficiency is such a complicated phenomenon that, short of an omniscient economist, a thorough accounting may never transpire. Even if there were such an omniscient one, he or she probably wouldn't find it efficient to invest the time in such labyrinthic detail.

Yet obvious cases of increased efficiency do exist, like computer technology. More efficient computers enable more efficiency in virtually all economic sectors. But that brings us to another question surrounding efficiency: What does the efficiency produce? E-mail, for example, allows us to communicate without using as much paper, ink, and postal service. It therefore allows us to communicate without using as much pulp, dye, and petroleum. That is clearly a good thing (unless perhaps you are in the pulp, dye, or petroleum industry). But the act of communication itself does nothing to grow or shrink the economy. *If* the communication is used to advertise a good or a service, *then* more efficient communication will lead to more production and consumption of the good or service. So when we hear talk about how we have progressed from an agricultural to an industrial to an information economy, a "megatrend" for the ages, we should at least question what the information is used for. If it is not used to produce goods or services, then that is quite fine, but it may not be said to contribute to economic growth. If it is used to produce goods and services, then it may be said to contribute to economic growth, which might be a dubious distinction as the limit to growth looms.

If you've ever purchased a train ticket, you can probably recall having two concerns: where the train was going, and how fast the train would take you there. And those concerns are clearly listed in order of importance. The direction of the train matters most; speed is only helpful if the direction is correct. If we find that we are going in the wrong direction, or worse yet on a *runaway* train regardless of direction, we might savor every clank of inefficiency the old train can impede itself with.

Finding it hard to maintain convincing arguments based on substitutability and efficiency, neoclassical economists have turned increasingly to the concept of "human capital" to back their claims of perpetual economic growth. Human capital is jargon for intelligence, education, and knowledge. So, when a new factory opens, it does not start from scratch, reinventing wheels and pulleys and conveyor belts. Instead, its owners start with a stock of knowledge derived from all the mistakes that were made by their predecessors in the industry. Neither will they achieve perfection, and their mistakes and the documentation thereof will help to instruct future factory owners. Libraries, universities, trade schools: all the institutions of science and technology will contribute to a more efficient production of goods and services.

There's that word efficiency again, and let not the redundancy go unnoticed. What can human capital be expected to achieve if not more ingenious efficiency or substitutions of resources? Greater ethics? A higher spiritual plane? Perhaps, but while these may produce a more equitable wealth distribution, they do not produce economic growth. In fact, these developments are just as likely to temper economic growth, as we will see in part 2. And so we find that the concept of human capital, namely the type of human capital that is employed for economic growth, is a fancy representation of the older concepts of substitutability and efficiency.

At this point, the neoclassical theory of economic growth starts to take on a Ptolemaic tarnish. Ptolemy was the revered Alexandrian astronomer, mathematician, and geographer who based his astronomy on the belief that all heavenly bodies revolve around the earth. In the second century A.D. when Ptolemy practiced, who could have thought otherwise? Ptolemy's portrayal of the universe was consistent with casual observation and official Church doctrine. There were inconsistencies with Ptolemy's model right from the start, but Ptolemy and his disciples were adept at explaining such irregularities with epicycles, deferents, equants, and eccentrics. As the centuries wore on, these geometric rationalizations got a bit unwieldy. By the latter part of the Middle Ages, Ptolemy's model resembled a short-circuited funhouse at the county fair. Along came Copernicus, the planets were seen at last to move around the sun, and the whole Ptolemaic system came crashing down in a pile of bells and whistles, leaving as its legacy a metaphor for futility. Thus with the neoclassical model of economic growth, at least as it pertains to growth limits.

There is much utility in neoclassical economics, to be sure. Owing to the toil of its practitioners, we have never known as much about the effects of interest rates on investment, the role of entrepreneurs in stimulating industry, the nature of competition in a free market system, the forms and fiascos of taxation, or the causes of inflation. But when it comes to economic growth, and particularly the limitations thereof, the neoclassical model with its infinite substitutability, ever-increasing efficiency, and redundant conceptualization of human capital is hardly Copernican.

# 3

# WHAT WILL THEY THINK OF NEXT, AND WHY?

Substitutability, efficiency, and human capital have been the bulwarks of the neoclassical theory that economic growth may continue in perpetuity. As these concepts are exposed to the realities of limited materials and productive space, diminishing returns to efficiency, and absorptive capacity for pollutants, we can expect neoclassical economists to do two things. Eventually they will recharge their arguments about substitutability and efficiency by resorting to the topic of space travel. But first, I suspect, they will devise new concepts to apply to an Earth-bound economy. And my guess is that their new concepts will have much to do with the services sector. Before we explore these likely frontiers in neoclassical thought, however, let us deal with the question of *why* the neoclassical economists continually rationalize their way to perpetual economic growth. Why keep piling on the bells and whistles? Why not just give up and admit that there is a limit, that there are abundant signs of our approaching the limit, and that better public service might be achieved by facing the limit and its implications for society?

As a caveat, it should be noted that there are economists who have done precisely that. Virtually by definition, though, these economists are no longer neoclassical. Neoclassical economics is too firmly invested in the perpetuity of economic growth for its practitioners to acknowledge growth limits. I have already alluded to the "radical" economists who dare speak of limits, and one more time I shall defer my discussion of them and their theory to chapter 5. For now, let us limit our discussion to the traditional neoclassical school, which remains the dominant establishment in academic economics and virtually the only establishment in applied economics.

One more caveat is in order. Not all economists of the neoclassical school deal with economic growth. Economics is one of the largest disciplines of our times, with an impressive array of specialties. The most basic distinction is between microeconomics and macroeconomics. Microeconomists deal with individual markets and with the determination of relative prices within those markets. Supply and demand of all goods and services lies within the realm of microeconomics. Macroeconomics is the study of the economy as a whole, and thus encompasses aggregate issues like inflation, unemployment, and economic growth. However, just as the microbiologist's curriculum often includes the basics of population ecology, the microeconomist's curriculum typically includes the basics of economic growth. Virtually all economists are united by a set of neoclassical theories that transcend the micro/macro distinction.

While one neoclassical economist focuses on the price of

beans in Arizona, another delves into international exchange rates. Some specialize in economic growth; these we call growth economists (some of whom distinguish themselves as Keynesian —here we refer to them all as neoclassical). It is probably safe to say, however, that the other economists in the United States, if pressed into reciting their beliefs about economic growth, would attempt to summarize the concepts of their neoclassical growth brethren. And that is to be expected, as the same phenomenon transpires in all fields. Wildlife ecologists, if pressed into an explanation of the origin of species, will recite what they recall of neo-Darwinian evolution. Galactic astronomers, if pressed into providing a model of planetary movements, will recite what they recall of neo-Copernican cosmology. Molecular geneticists pressed into explaining the inheritance of physical traits will recite what they recall of neo-Mendelian heredity. All specialists are familiar with the theories of their classical predecessors and at least vaguely familiar with the neoclassical syntheses thereof. So I will retain the convention of attributing the dominant paradigm, that of unlimited economic growth potential, simply to neoclassical economics or, alternatively, to neoclassical econo*mists*, with the understanding that, strictly speaking, the dominant paradigm is championed by neoclassical *growth* economists.

Championed in academia, at least. But most Americans, steeped in democracy and majority rule, understand the pervasiveness of politics. And they understand the influence of business on political affairs. Who then would benefit politically by an economic growth theory that embraces infinite potential? Pick an industry, any industry. From the street corner pop stand to Coca Cola itself, every business would like to sell twice as much, be it goods or services. If it can get help from the government, so much the better. But government is supposed to do what is right for society as a whole, not assist one legitimate interest at the expense of another. So isn't it convenient to have a theory that there is no limit to economic growth? That way, politicians are off the hook. They can simply provide support and encouragement to each and every business, and expect to have the support returned from each and every one at election time. That pretty much explains the embrace of neoclassical growth theory by politicians.

As for the neoclassical economists themselves, they face strong deterrents to heading off in other directions. They are like scientists in all established fields who are instilled with established theory during their undergraduate studies and dutifully participate in continual reinforcement through rituals of examination, oration, and composition. They proceed to their graduate research, whereupon everything they investigate is interpreted from the perception of their undergraduate indoctrination. They find it difficult to see things any other way. Ptolemy's students and centuries of disciples were a prime example.

This phenomenon has long been noted by philosophers of science, with Thomas Kuhn providing the classic account in *The Structure of Scientific Revolutions.* Kuhn thought that knowledge was perceived from views, or "paradigms," which were reconstructed only during scientific revolutions, and not during "normal science." Kuhn (1996:121) noted that more than one interpretation can always be derived from a given collection of data, and that, "with a change of paradigm, the scientist afterward works in a different world." After Copernicus, astronomers lived in a world that revolved around the sun. After Columbus, navigators lived in a world that was round. Of course, everyone else had always lived in a round world that revolved around the sun, at least all the non-indoctrinated, common folk. Only when we have a more Copernican economics will economists live in a world in which economic growth is limited, where the rest of us common folk are already stuck.

In addition to the deterrence of doctrine, neoclassical economists face personal and professional incentives for perpetuating and strengthening neoclassical growth theory. Like all scientists, they advance by getting scientific journal articles published, so they do themselves a favor by submitting manuscripts that don't buck the system. A scientist who submits a maverick manuscript has to be prepared to muster twice the evidence, to do twice the work to get it published. All else equal, that means that mavericks will get half as many articles published. The system-bucking articles that they manage to get published will put them under the microscope. They can expect scathing reviews and letters to editors. Future manuscript submissions may be viewed with inordinate scrutiny. Colleagues may shun them. If they continue down this path, they may find themselves ostracized by their professional colleagues. Research funds may dry up, and their careers may be destroyed.

Furthermore, the incentives faced by politicians and neoclassical economists do not function independently. No one should be surprised by the power of politics in education and research. We see it on the news all the time. Some poor science teacher wants to incorporate the topic of evolution and gets waylaid by the religious right. In the next county another teacher wants to incorporate divine creation and gets waylaid by the nonreligious left. All they have to do is swap counties and they'll get by. But how hard must it be for the poor schlunk who wants to incorporate the limits to economic growth, with every businessman and politician in the country in the other corner, waving thousands of journal articles authored by conventional neoclassicists? And that's assuming the poor schlunk ever made it onto a faculty to begin with.

Academia is supposed to be the place where thinking is free, socially conscious yet liberated from all concerns not scientific or philosophical. A place where thinkers are hired regardless of such concerns. And it probably fits that description better than any other endeavor. But better is not the same as extensively.

I remember my first interview for an assistant professor position. It was at one of the largest universities in the nation, a renowned institution that resides in an ultra-conservative, economically booming region. The hiring committee had already interviewed two candidates for the position, and decided that neither fit the bill. So I was called in with the encouraging words, "The door is wide open." During my three days on campus, I met with everyone from the dean of the college to the freshmen in the halls. I was toured around town while one professor's wife, who was also a realtor, tried to sell me a house. On the second day I presented my teaching seminar, for which I received gracious praise. Later at dinner with the department chairman, we talked about future prospects and discussed salary.

On the third day I presented my research seminar. Sticking with tradition, I presented the results of my doctoral research —my policy analysis of the Endangered Species Act. In fact, the presentation was virtually identical to my dissertation defense, and I had given the talk to several other audiences, so I couldn't help but have it down pat. Although I've delivered my share of junky presentations, in this case I had aesthetically pleasing slides, a logical organization, and rich data of national import, including the results of a nationwide public opinion survey. I also provided my analysis of the causes of species endangerment on the mainland United States. Urbanization, agriculture, outdoor recreation and tourism, domestic livestock and ranching activities, reservoirs and other water diversions, modified fire regimes, pollution, mineral/oil/gas exploration and extraction, logging, industrial development, roads, aquifer depletion, and a few other causes, with numbers of endangered species listed alongside. This "Who's Who" of American economy, I pointed out, comprised the economic context of the Endangered Species Act (ESA, for short). The results of this analysis had already been summarized in *Science* (Czech and Krausman 1997).

And then I came to my recommendations, the final and, as I emphasized, the ultimate one being, "There are only two possible policy recommendations for alleviating the ESA/context paradox: Abandon the goal of ESA or abandon the goal of economic growth." Jaws commenced to dropping and jobs commenced to walking. (Actually, some jaws had commenced to dropping a few minutes earlier, when I gave them the good old Jack Kemp quote.) Of course, I wasn't suicidal enough to leave it at that. I acknowledged the political barriers to either alternative, and I proceeded to make some cautious, correlated recommendations. But it was too late. "Well Brian, it's been nice having you here," the department chairman said on the walk back to department headquarters. Now I cannot scientifically prove that my critique of economic growth lost me the job, but if you doubt it highly, maybe they still have some swampland (or a supposed substitute thereof) for sale in Florida.

About a month later, I got a call from another, much smaller university in the same region. They were considering whether or not to invite me for an interview. The search committee chair asked what I thought of the Endangered Species Act—of all people to ask! He informed me that they had sort of an informal agreement with the ranchers in the region whereby faculty, upon encountering an endangered species in the field, would make no mention of the finding. Needless to say, that didn't get anywhere.

Such has been my personal experience, but again, common sense dictates that political interests invade the academic sphere. And the venerable economist-historian, John Kenneth Galbraith, has long described such an invasion in the economics discipline. Economists, academic and bureaucratic, are hired to toe the line for economic interests. Rarely explicitly, but almost always effectively.

Now imagine an aspiring professor of economics who denies the infinitude of substitutability attempting to land a job at a university receiving millions of dollars of grant money from extractive industries. And when you look around, there aren't too many universities that don't receive such funding. The point of all this is that one should not be surprised to find that those economists who acknowledge a limit to economic growth are a very small minority, and one cannot conclude that their minority status makes them in any way less correct. Indeed, their minority status is simply an indicator of where the power lies and what the power wants. That's why I call them radical economists.

Now that we have outlined the reasons *why* neoclassical economists are compelled to build upon the Ptolemaic theory of perpetual economic growth, we may ponder *what* they may come up with next. As I earlier alluded, the services sector appears ripe for their attention. That is because services, per se, do not consume resources. When one purchases services, one purchases expertise, even if only of the mundane type. So the concept of increasing human capital goes hand in hand with growth of the services sector.

The argument says that, over time, the proportion of services to goods increases. And once again, this is laden with common sense and backed by historical fact. We used to be a nation of farmers. Most common folk and even much of the upper class were farmers in the 1700s and early 1800s. As the population grew and farming communities became more dense, towns sprang up and entrepreneurial folks offered their services to the farmers. The proverbial butchers, bakers, and candlestick makers. They didn't require much land to ply their trade. Goods were brought to them, and their services transformed those goods into value-added goods, thus entailing a profit for the service providers.

Now we can see the first flaw in the services argument for infinite economic growth. Even the services require goods, and the resale of those goods (with added value), for their existence. The butcher and the candlestick maker depended on the farmer who raised cattle and pigs, while the baker depended on the farmer who grew wheat and oats. To "produce" more T-bones or candles required more cattle and pigs. To "produce" more bread required more wheat and oats. It is easy to see why François Quesnay and the so-called physiocrats (predecessors of the classical economists, prominent in France in the 1760s) argued that agriculture was the sole source of economic production and growth. That is how Thomas Jefferson saw it, too.

Of course, as the Industrial Revolution unfolded, the production of various manufactured goods was tied to the availability of all types of new servicing. Products useful for urbanization, especially, required mass services like transportation and construction. Again it is easy to see how these services cannot be performed without the consumption of goods, like pine boards and aluminum studs. If we expand the concept of agriculture to include all types of extraction from the earth, we see again that the physiocrats made a compelling point.

However, as time went on and the economy flourished, providing large numbers of people with profits and leisure time, some services came into vogue that didn't seem to require many resources at all. People wanted entertainment, so some folks got paid to paint paintings, dance, and write scripts. Of course, even these services required tiny bits of resources, like the paint for paintings, the dresses for dancing, and the pages for scripts. But, as the neoclassical economist will point out, we see a major reduction in the amount of resources required—such a reduction, in fact, as to make the resources required appear insignificant.

Theoretically, of course, even a seemingly insignificant use of resources is limited by the amount of resources available, so that economic growth based on such services could not be viewed as possessing infinite potential. We would not, for example, have enough paint to produce a billion zillion paintings. But the neoclassical economist can point out that it is the *proportion* of services to goods that allows for infinite economic growth potential. The conversion of one farmer, whose existence is based on using hundreds of acres of land, makes way for a great many painters, the existence of each being based on a studio and tiny bits of product from the land.

At the heart of this argument is that ever elaborate notion of efficiency. In a nation with growing population, the only way to convert another farmer into a bunch of painters is to make the remaining farms more efficient. That used to be easy, when there was plenty of fertile frontier available for plowing. Those days are long gone. Today, expanding the agricultural land base requires the employment of ever less productive lands. At the dry end of the spectrum, it means we have to build more dams or drill more wells (as into the Oglala aquifer) to supply irrigation water. At the wet end of the spectrum, it means we have to drain more wetlands (as with the Everglades) to supply tillable soil.

The neoclassical economist will argue that increases in efficiency are not limited to the land, however. More efficient methods, like intensive tillage, irrigation, and fertilizing, will allow for more production with less acreage farmed. Now we come full circle to the nuances of efficiency, which we have already discussed and discounted. Just to be safe, let it be said here that more intensive farming leads to soil erosion, more intensive irrigation depends on more water and degrades soil by depositing salts, and more intensive fertilizing requires the mining of more natural gas and phosphate rock. All of these phenomena lead to less productive capacity of the land. And all require more petroleum, the trump card facing the player of the efficiency hand.

The neoclassical economist may finally argue that, through genetic technology, we will design ever more productive crops. Well, right now, a world class high jumper can perhaps clear a world class stalk of sweet corn. Will tomorrow's jumper of fifty feet, assuming he evolves, find a fifty-foot stalk of corn to clear? And will that fifty-foot stalk of corn find a suitably deep, damp, and fertile soil layer to support it? Perhaps great advances in crop production await, as with hydroponic (soilless) farming, but to say they have no bounds is to ignore the laws of nature.

Getting back to the services sector, then, we see that only a limited number of farmers are available for conversion to services. The rest will have to stick to farming, or those of us not trained to survive in the wild—assuming there is any wild left—will starve.

Here is where a little training in the natural sciences would benefit economics. Biologists who deal with the economy of nature employ a handy concept called trophic levels. The participants in the economy of nature are other species, each of which exists on some level based upon their productive capacity. At the bottom level are the true producers, the plants which take oxygen from the air and water from the soil and produce their own food. They were endowed with chlorophyll to pull this off. In fact, they produce surplus food which may be used by other species. They also produce goods like straw for nests and sticks for dams. They are the "farmers" and other goods producers in the economy of nature. Virtually nothing else lives without them.

At the next level, we have the primary consumers, the animals which eat and otherwise use plants to survive. Carpenter ants and beavers, for example. We might consider them the working class of nature's society—the carpenters and dam builders and such. They in turn provide nutrition for the next level, the secondary consumers like spiders and bobcats. We might view these species as the capitalists of nature, moving through the ecosystem looking for cheaper labor like colonies of laboring ants or pools of laboring beavers to prey upon. At the highest level are the super carnivores, the mega-predators like mountain lions that depend on big primary consumers like deer and even small secondary consumers like bobcats. We might consider them the wealthy class, the "fat cats" of nature's society. Throughout this economy we have service providers like bees that pollinate plants, worms that till soil, and scavengers that clean up the mess, much like the sanitation services in our human economy.

None of the secondary consumers would exist were it not for the primary consumers, and none of the fat cats would exist were it not for both of the former. The service providers would not exist were it not for the species for which they provide their services. And clearly, none of the other species—not even the sponges— would exist were it not for the farmers and other goods producers. In any economy, someone has to produce before anyone can consume. In that sense, the physiocrats were right on.

As a corollary, there is a certain *amount* of production required to support the current population of primary consumers. And there is a certain population of primary consumers required to support the current population of secondary consumers, and a certain population of secondary consumers to support the current population of super carnivores. Certain populations of each are required to support the population of servicers. One way to support more, at any level, is to increase the population at the next lower level, which in turn requires an increase at the next lower level; ultimately, an increase in (plant) production is required. "All mortals are grass," proclaimed the prophet Isaiah (Isaiah 40:6). The only other way to support a larger economy of nature is to increase the efficiency operating in any given level. In other words, the animals in that level have to produce more young with the same amount of resources availed to them from the next lower level.

Now nothing can match God, Mother Nature, and four billion years of evolving life when it comes to increasing efficiency. Giraffes' necks surpass the agility and leverage of the most expensive cranes, hummingbird hearts purr more reliably than the tiniest motors, and our most advanced fighter jets can't rival the poetic lethality of the peregrine's dive. If you've ever seen a mountain lion dispatch an unsuspecting mule deer, you've seen the epitome of efficiency. The economy of nature led the British philosopher David Hume to observe:

> Look round the world, contemplate the whole and every part of it: you will find . . . [that all] these various machines, and even their most minute parts, are adjusted to each other with an accuracy which ravishes into admiration all men who have ever contemplated them. The curious adapting of means to ends, throughout all nature, resembles exactly, though it much exceeds, the production of human contrivance (quoted in Cronin 1991 : 12).

Yet the point comes over the eons, as it has several times in paleoecological history, where these wondrous adaptations do nothing to add to the total *number* of animals in the economy of nature, nor the total *mass* thereof. Instead, these adaptations are all about out-*competing* other species and individuals. We are told that this has been so at least since the Cambrian period, when the leisurely evolution of the Precambrian era went by the way about 600 million years ago: "Competition was introduced into ecology . . . When this changed, it changed for ever. Indeed, competitiveness still governs all biological life" (Fortey 1998 : 101). In the economy of nature the types of goods and services may change, but the mass of animal flesh is limited by the amount of producers available for consumption, who in turn are limited by the amount of water, oxygen, and sunlight available to them. And in terms of sunlight, the amount available is not just a function of solar radiation (the ultimate limiting factor), but also the ability to out-compete other plants for access to that sunlight. In other words, the economy of nature may be ultimately limited by the availability of solar radiation, but is more proximately limited by the space available on Earth.

The economy of nature is more than just an analogy to the human economy. After all, humans are a part of nature. Regardless of our spiritual distinctiveness, in our physical manifestation we are a species that is subject to the same laws of nature as all others. So we can have a great diversity of consumers, fat cats, and service providers, but the scale of all their activity is limited by goods production. "The farmer," whether it be one giant corporation or millions of family farms, is the source of food for all. Companion producers of goods, like miners and loggers, are the sources of all other goods. The economy can only get so efficient, and then it grows no more.

Perhaps this limited proportions principle underlies the lament of the Emmy Award–winning reporter Jeffrey Madrick (1995:60): "the productivity gains of the huge services sector have slowed to a virtual crawl where once they had risen rapidly." After all, services already account for 80 percent of gross domestic product, while raw materials account for less than 7 percent. And most of our raw materials have to be imported; our trade deficit doesn't derive from our employment of foreign services! Furthermore, one of the traditional sources of efficiency—corporate research—has been culled out of the system as profits have diminished alongside the productivity of services.

Given the limited proportions principle, it also comes as no surprise that the growth rate of the goods sector exceeds that of the services sector during expansion phases of the American economy (Hamrin 1988). The significance of this finding may be complicated to some extent by foreign trade developments, but it is certainly consistent with the trophic reality that real growth comes from the bottom up. When the bottom stops growing, the growth rate of the top may continue for awhile, until the proportional limit is reached. When the bottom just can't grow any more, the proportional limit amounts to an absolute limit.

Apparently a cadre of economic "structuralists" were on to the concept of trophic levels as early as 1940 when Colin Clark (who had a natural science background) described economies in terms of primary, secondary, and tertiary sectors. But the structuralists held little sway among the dominant, neoclassical school. (See W. W. Rostow's *Theorists of Economic Growth from David Hume to the Present* for an account of the structural/neoclassical confrontation.) And more elaborate neoclassical arguments lie ahead, as some services may seem to approach true independence from natural resource consumption. As an example, let us return to the so-called information economy. Information is not a physical good but a mental construct. Those who invest their efforts in such construction are providing a service. When we buy information, we are paying for the mental strain of the provider. People these days are buying information left and right, and when they buy it over the Internet, who can say that resources are consumed in the process? The best we can argue in a conventional sense is that these information providers must eat and drink, and perhaps use some petroleum to travel around in the quest for compiling data.

But there is a more compelling, if unconventional argument, based on the utility of the information. If the information is useful for producing more goods and services at competitive prices, its purchase is justified in an economic sense, and it becomes part of the process of production. For example, if the information consists of a plan for building a new factory, and the information is employed, then a new factory will be built, with the plan factored into the capital outlay. Obviously such a sequence does nothing to evade the limit to growth faced by the industry in question.

True, one can purchase information just for yuks. Literally, as when one purchases a list of jokes. But unless one employs a wildly esoteric argument (based perhaps on motivational value), can the jokes be seen as doing something real to grow the economy? They provide no one with food, clothing, shelter, convenience, or economically relevant information. Yet they were purchased, with the purchase price contributing to gross national product.

Of this sector of yuks, indeed of the entire mental services sector, one may wonder, where does the money to purchase such services come from? And again it can readily be seen that the money comes ultimately from the lowest trophic levels—the producers of goods. The money may pass through the hands of manufacturers, bankers, and many others along the way, but it comes from an agricultural surplus.

If Adam Smith were alive today, he would set the record straight. He would show, just as he did in *Wealth of Nations*, how money originated via division of labor. And what freed the hands for labor so divided? Agricultural surplus. No agricultural surplus, no money. If everyone wrote jokes, there would be no money to buy them. Or, if money was already in the economy from prior agricultural surplus, but we found that our money was now good only for yuks, the money would become worthless. People would drop their joke books and head back to the farm. Otherwise they would die laughing in the sector of yuks like King Midas died of starvation after surrounding himself with piles of inedible gold.

Although the primacy of agricultural surplus is shrouded today by a fog of paper money and financial hocus-pocus, the principle still applies. The economy has a limited capacity for joke writers and all other mental service providers. That capacity is determined by the amount of agricultural and other goods available to the economy. So we see that the services sector, even the mental services sector, is limited by the goods sector, which is limited by the amount of resources on Earth. Perpetually increasing the proportion of services to goods in the economy depends on a perpetually increasing production of goods, which is impossible. So the services sector does not offer the prospect of unlimited economic growth.

Today, only 18 percent of the American labor force actually produces goods. More than a fourth is devoted to exchanging things; these are the wholesalers, retailers, bankers, realtors, and the like. Most of the rest work for Uncle Sam or stand in the welfare line. A few dance and write jokes. The professor of economics who tabulated these figures, Kenneth E. Boulding, agreed that the reduction of the agricultural work force was a result of technological efficiency. He also ventured that "these labour-saving improvements have clearly reached their limit" (Boulding 1993: 22). He wasn't sure how close the manufacturing sector had come to its limits.

Now that the neoclassical bulwarks of substitutability, efficiency, and human capital have been laid aside, and the perpetual expansion of the services sector has been obviated, we may soon turn back to the economy of nature for some valuable lessons. Perhaps in nature there resides a Copernican economics, a replacement for the Ptolemaic neoclassical economic growth theory. First, however, let's take one last look at neoclassical growth theory by focusing on one of its all-time champions in popular culture, Julian Simon.

# 4

# SIMON SAID

Much of chapters 2 and 3 could be classified as theoretical, but I prefer to classify it as common sense. And, when you think about it, there is a fine line between theory and common sense. Both are constructed with bits and pieces of knowledge, variable amounts of reasoning, and generous doses of observation. Common sense is the working man's repository of theory. But not everyone is enamored with common sense. Julian Simon, for example, was fond of exhorting his readers to avoid its distractions. While touting the infinitude of natural resource supplies in his book *Ultimate Resource 2* he admitted, "I realize that this approach probably still seems so anti-commonsensical as to be beyond belief, but please read on. Like many other important complex questions, this one can be understood only by coming to see the sense in what seems at first to be pure foolishness" (p. 43). I for one did read on, eagerly and hopefully—the whole 734 pages' worth—and shall dutifully report my observations.

But first, who was Julian Simon? He was a professor of business administration at the University of Maryland and a senior fellow at the Cato Institute (a right-wing think tank that shows up on lists of anti-environmental organizations). He was a prolific author of academic and popular articles and books, and a well-traveled speaker. He was perhaps the most influential proponent of unlimited economic growth of all time. His life's work culminated with the 1996 publication of *Ultimate Resource 2*, which relied heavily upon thirty-seven of his earlier publications and came complete with a tribute by Nobel Prize–winning economist Milton Friedman.

Judging by the preface to *Ultimate Resource 2*, Simon had warm qualities and was driven to the study of economics out of a concern for human welfare. He liked the outdoors but was comfortable in society. He loved life and wanted more folks to experience it in comfort. And, although he promoted consumption, he despised waste. I would like to have met the man, who unfortunately died during the year I wrote this book. He was the prototypical optimist, and for his optimism I admire him posthumously.

Nevertheless, as a treatise on economic growth, *Ultimate Resource 2* was immensely disappointing, and I found myself unable to participate in Simon's version of optimism. This was partly a function of misleading facts, such as, "the quantity of land [in the United States] under cultivation has been decreasing" (p. 6), despite the fact that agricultural acreage (including cropland and animal production land) had increased from approximately 958 million acres in 1920 to 981 million acres in 1992 (Cramer and Jensen 1994). To Simon's credit, he was insistent on considering the longest time frame possible. "The intellectual practice of focusing on a very short period which runs against the long-term trend—but which fits with one's preconceptions—has been the most frequent cause of error in understanding the relationship of natural resources to population growth and human progress" (p. 112). Unfortunately, he paid scant attention to his own insistence. For example, he neglected to mention that since pre-Columbian days the increase in agricultural acreage would have been all 981 million acres (minus the relatively small amount cultivated by the Native Americans). This *truly* long-term and simple observation is all that is required to negate Simon's claim that agricultural acreage decreases over the long term, even with expanding populations, as production becomes more efficient.

When Simon cited a 1984 Department of Agriculture press release which averred that "The average annual rate of soil erosion on cultivated cropland dropped from 5.1 tons per acre to 4.8 tons per acre" (p. 147), he made no mention of the time frame whatsoever, and provided no published citation that would allow the time frame to be checked. The press release may very well have been an annual report that provided a two-year time series. After all, authorities were simultaneously concurring that the phenomenon was worsening throughout the world in step with economic growth (Brown and Wolf 1984). If erosion rates decline in the future, it could simply be the result of an already depleted base from which the soil may erode.

Some of Simon's "facts" were not only misleading but scarcely substantiated. He noted that the world fish catch had leveled off in the 1970s, but that "by 1988 the catch had reached 98 million tons a year, and it is still increasing rapidly. . . . No limit to the harvest of wild varieties of seafood is in sight" (p. 104). Here he was talking about the catch of wild varieties, not the harvest of aquacultured fish, and his claim seems astounding with all we hear about oceanic fish stocks becoming depleted. Where did he get

such a fish story? He cited as his source "Wise, forthcoming"—
in other words, an unpublished source unavailable for examination. (Twelve years earlier, John P. Wise had authored a chapter
on the world's supply of fish, in a book edited by Simon and Herman Kahn called *The Resourceful Earth*. Apparently Simon was
calling on Wise one more time.) Yet the years following 1988 have
exhibited a well-documented decline in world fish catch due to
overfishing, destructive fishing methods (like "biomass trawlers"
that scrape the ocean floor), pollution, and coastal development
(Bulloch 1989, Kane 1993).

Neoclassical fish stories are catchy (pardon the pun) in the
popular press. They tend to extend to other denizens of the seas.
The science (and science fiction) writer Adrian Berry (1996:111)
noted that, just as there are two main types of farming on land,
"so it will be in the sea. The crops will be seaweed. . . . The cattle
will be whales." With eleven of the fifteen major oceanic fisheries in decline (Brown et al. 1999), whales may indeed be next
on the list—for consumption, that is. But those among us who
can stomach the meat of these highly intelligent mammals may
have a stiff price to pay—whales have already undergone a well-
documented decline due to the whale oil market. In fact, all the
large species are endangered.

Simon quoted from the journal *Regulation*—hardly a bastion
of science—that "low-level radiations make the cells less susceptible to subsequent high doses of radiation" (p. 207). He called
this a "fact" and used it to support his conclusion that "it is possible to have *too little* exposure to radiation" (emphasis in the original). Simon also got his money's worth from newspapers, which
he frequently used as sources of information on scientific topics. He brushed away issues of atmospheric stability by reasoning,

"the newspapers are reporting 'Greenhouse Effect Seems Benign So Far,' and similar news about the ozone effect. So much for the two great scares of the early 1990s" (p. 272). For Simon, all it took was a few news articles to trump Roan's (1989) *Ozone Crisis* (to give just one example), a 270-page book of theoretical and empirical evidence for ozone depletion and global warming.

In addition to news articles, Simon's sources included many unpublished documents—letters, draft reports, and documents simply cited as "xeroxes"—and a large amount of "personal correspondence." Some of his endnotes even referred to publications that cannot be found in his list of references. Although I found it necessary to cross-check only a small fraction of his endnotes, I ran across this problem three times (endnotes 11 and 12 of chapter 19 and endnote 19 of chapter 21). Presumably there are many more such phantom citations. For problems like this, of course, the publishing company should share the blame with the author.

Worse yet, many of Simon's "facts" had *no* substantiation—not even phantomized—despite periodic claims that all we had to do to believe these incredible facts was to check his data sources. For many of his figures (line graphs, bar charts, and the like), it is impossible to ascertain where the data came from; only educated guesses may be made. Without substantiation Simon claimed, "There is practically zero chance of a nuclear-plant catastrophe that would cost tens of thousands of lives. The very outside possibility envisioned by the official committees of experts is a catastrophe causing five thousand deaths" (p. 208). What committees? We'll never know. Simon also asserted that "the problem of safeguarding the processed [nuclear] waste from year to year is much less difficult than is safeguarding the national gold supply at Fort Knox" (p. 205). Says who? Simon didn't say. Supposedly, "All now agree that the 1980s forecasts of the sea rising many inches or feet due to global warming are nonsense" (p. 188). Apparently, when you know what "all" think, you don't have to cite them.

Simon also employed his "facts" fallaciously. For example, he cited the immense wealth of Switzerland, Holland, and Hong Kong as evidence for the diminishing economic importance of land and goods production. Yet who with a modest knowledge of world history is unaware that these countries accumulated their wealth by the colonization of resource-rich lands (Holland), investment of resource-rich countries (Hong Kong), and financial wizardry on the world markets in which resource-rich countries conduct business (Switzerland). Not to mention the fact that the international forays of Holland were originally enabled by the agricultural wealth of her own lands.

Simon must have read neither Rondo Cameron's (1989) *Economic History of the World* nor Michael Barratt Brown's (1995) *Models in Political Economy*. Brown pointed out that, "In no industrialized country have living standards been raised without a base of competitive industry. This is true even of Switzerland . . . " (p. 82). And, "Even Switzerland, which is often quoted as the supreme example of a successful service economy, depending on tourism and banking, has in fact always maintained a highly competitive export business in precision instruments and machine tools. While there was a great increase in world trade in services in the 1980s, it no more than kept up with world trade in goods" (p. 115).

Even with facts that might not be disputed or fallaciously employed, Simon's interpretations of them are not exactly heartwarming. For example, we are told that our worries about nuclear fallout are unwarranted, because in a study of cancer in 100,000

Japanese subjects following the World War II atomic bomb blasts, "about one hundred more have developed leukemia than would be otherwise expected, and about three hundred more than expected have developed solid cancers—a total of four hundred" (p. 205). Extrapolating this effect to the population of the United States, for example, the additional cases of cancer would only be slightly over one million, so why worry about large-scale fallout? Later, Simon mentioned a Danish study entitled, "Big Drop in Sperm Count since '38," but declined a technical discussion of it and offered instead (p. 259), "Would anyone care to bet on whether this new scare turns out to be valid?" No risk aversion there!

When the facts couldn't be molded to fit his argument, Simon simply made up his own terminology. For example, he insisted that pollution had been decreasing all along, not increasing. He said we should gauge pollution by life expectancy—if life expectancy was increasing, pollution had to be decreasing. Never mind the contributions to life expectancy of nutritional, medical, and diplomatic expertise; "pollution has been declining since the beginning of the species" (p. 233), simply because life expectancy has increased. This disregard for causality is supplemented by Simon's reinvention of the word "pollution" to include "bones cast aside after meals" in prior millennia (p. 233), "infectious diseases such as pneumonia, tuberculosis, and gastroenteritis" in recent centuries (p. 236), and even "crime in the streets" today (p. 240)!

Such conceptual impertinence in the pursuit of economic growth is commonplace, especially in the "pop economics" literature. How about this classic: "A simple example will show how profound are the consequences of moving from average growth of 3.2% to 2.3%. If a pilot made a navigational error of equal magnitude in charting a flight east from New York to Moscow, the plane would end up somewhere over the middle of the Black Sea." Who came up with this "profound" observation? Jack Kemp! Perhaps Kemp (1998:16) was recalling an errant pass from his stint with the Buffalo Bills.

But back to Simon, whose view of resource scarcity depended entirely on price trends—a view that would be hotly contested from the grandkids' discounted perspective. Because prices for many natural resources had fallen over the decades, Simon insisted that the resources were actually becoming *more* abundant in an economic sense—the only sense that should matter. As fellow optimist Ronald Bailey (1996:129) reminded those who must have forgotten, "As we all know, falling prices mean that goods are becoming more abundant, not more scarce." Simon was convinced by his self-christened "grand theory" that "If humankind had not evolved patterns of behavior that increased rather than decreased the amounts of resources available to us, we would not still be here" (p. 74), despite the commonsense recognition that humans began their existence in a world full of resources and are now finally arriving at the point where shortages appear. Simon also neglected the fact that modern machinery has made it easier to unearth resources, thus making them cheaper in the short term but prone to exhaustion even sooner. There was no reason, as he saw it, to predict a resource shortage when decades of prices were moving in the opposite direction or stabilized.

Yet other scholars have noted the simplest of mechanisms for reconciling price stability and resource shortage. As Virginia Abernethy (1991:6) observed, "fewer and fewer people will be in the market to buy them. More people will go without." Overpopulation and poverty, in other words, would keep effective demand down, because the demands of destitute people would have no economic impact. Richard Norgaard (1990) even identified a fallacy associated with using prices to reflect resource shortages. He noted that using prices entailed the assumption that resource allocators are informed of resource scarcity. In other words, if extractors and wholesalers knew that resources were becoming scarce, they would raise prices. Yet how would they know? Presumably not based on prices, since they were the ones responsible for raising those. On the other hand, if they did not really know, then what would prices tell us about scarcity? Really not much. Many factors affect prices, and scarcity has little effect until perhaps it has reached ominous proportions.

Furthermore, there is no denying that food and other resource shortages have indeed plagued human populations around the globe for centuries. Simon denied the relationship of such shortages to ecological limitations, however, and put the onus on political economy instead. "Any country that gives to farmers a free market in food and labor, secure property rights in the land, and a political system that ensures these freedoms in the future will soon be flush with food, with an ever-diminishing proportion of its work force required to produce the food" (p. 109). This mistakes the cart for the horse, however, because the strongest democracies have flourished precisely where there were plenty of resources to begin with, with the United States providing the outstanding example. Simon could have gathered this lesson from common sense or from Brown's *Models in Political Economy.* Where intensive struggles for resources exist, one can expect bellicose behavior and dictatorial regimes, as in the desert nations in the Middle East and overpopulated countries like China. When resource-rich western nations had a democratic head start but later found themselves pinched by shortages as their economies grew, their least democratic behavior transpired outside their own borders, as in colonial times.

Simon's obsession with prices led him to view *people* as the economic factor in short supply. "This increase in the price of people's services is a clear indication that people are becoming more scarce even though there are more of us" (p. 40). He strove to vanquish fears about overpopulation, and saw no problem with tampering with the Earth's heat budget. If crop production as we know it today couldn't keep up with population growth, we could count on innovations like hydroponic farming and "orbiting giant mirrors that would reflect sunlight onto the night side of the Earth and thereby increase growing time" (p. 100). In fact, "The supply of energy is not even finite, and its price may be expected to fall forever" (p. 197).

Simon could have taken a page from *The Hopeful Future*, in which techno-optimist Harry Stine (1983:112) predicted, "we won't be using coal and petroleum for burning in the twenty-first century. . . . We'll find many energy solutions by 2001." To prove Stine right, we have one year to convert an economy that is nothing if not coal- and petroleum-burning. (Stine also claimed that we could expect cures for all known forms of cancer by 2001.) The faith in perpetually improving technology extends from the energy sector to the economy as a whole. Contributors to *The Rising Tide* argued that "technological innovation can raise the growth rate permanently and substantially" (Jasinowski 1998:xxiii).

A combination of convenient "fact" finding, fallacious reasoning, disregard for ecological consequences, market system myopia, and utopian leanings led Simon to observe, "there is no 'law' of diminishing returns in general" (p. 171), "there is no reason to believe that the future will be sharply different from the past" (p. 171), and "the supply of effective agricultural land can be expanded without limit" (p. 135). The latter was hardly relevant, however, because "the entire population of the world can be fed using only the land area of Massachusetts plus Vermont, or Netherlands plus Jamaica. And the area necessary can be reduced to a tenth or a hundredth of that by producing the food in ten- or hundred-story buildings" (p. 130).

Simon's neoclassical rationale begs the question: If an economy may grow perpetually on a specified land base—like Earth—could not a nongrowing but stable economy persist on a perpetually diminishing land base? Why stop at squishing the global agricultural sector into one building? Why not have the whole world economy—all sectors—operate in Missouri? Or one block of St. Louis? Or one building, closet, or empty tobacco canister?

Simon denigrated Thomas Malthus and his first book on population—"the Malthusian mother of all scares" (p. 260)—because population growth rates had actually slowed in recent years. Simon never acknowledged that Malthus's influence may have been instrumental in slowing the growth rates of Western civilization, nor that some countries have endured a very Malthusian experience. Nor did Simon acknowledge that his own "grand theory" borrowed considerably from Malthus himself. Malthus readily acknowledged that population pressures brought out the creativeness in humans; thus he said, "Had population and food increased in the same ratio, it is probable that man might never have emerged from the savage state" (from Hodgson 1996:64). Malthus just had the sense to recognize a limit to the extent of that emergence.

Simon even made a strawman of Karl Marx and his labor theory of value, alleging that Marx would not have accounted for the differential training of surgeons and janitors when ascribing the value of their respective labors. Could one such as Marx have lacked the insight that training itself comprised labor, which would therefore add immensely to the value of the surgeon's work? When it comes to the benefit of the doubt, Marx would have to merit more than Simon.

Perhaps it was sheer over-exuberance that led Simon to call John Maynard Keynes, "on the subject of natural resources . . . both ignorant of the facts and stupid" (p. 56).

Simon's strawman arguments were not applied exclusively to all-time economic geniuses. He claimed that "Ecologists seem to be calling for an economics-like science based on their own values, which include the points of view of other species" (p. 232). Here he tried, as many anti-environmental activists have done over the years, to portray ecology as united with the animal rights movement. Although there are ecologists (and economists) who are animal rightists, the percentage is very small. In fact, many ecologists—especially wildlife biologists—go into the profession because they like to hunt and fish. Common sense! Most ecologists (including myself) call for a new economics for the sake of the grandkids, not to safeguard animal rights.

Unfortunately, common sense itself is an effigy in Simon's gallery of strawmen. He lamented, " 'Common sense' argues that specific planning for particular kinds of outcomes results in a better general outcome than an undesigned system. Yet the evidence is incontrovertible that with respect to ordinary economic matters, an undesigned free-enterprise system does much better than does a planned Socialist system" (p. 306). Here we are subtly encouraged to believe not only that common sense has misled us again, but that economic planning is one and the same as socialism with a capital S, that dirty word that triggers paranoia in the American psyche. There is no recognition that all capitalist democracies have found it necessary to engage in various degrees of planning and regulation due to the complexities brought about by economic growth.

Simon tended to be very selective in his use of examples, sometimes transparently so. He asserted, "There is no evidence that public officials are better stewards of any class of property—including wilderness and parks—than are private owners" (p. 304). He conveniently neglected the classic examples of parks and wilderness saved from wholesale liquidation, like Yellowstone, Yosemite, and Acadia national parks. To support his assertion, he cited tiny Ravenna Park in Seattle, Washington, where apparently the city's takeover resulted in some illegal firewood cutting.

Simon provided a list of "definitely disproven threats" (pp. 260–265) that included land shortage, DDT, PCBs, malathion, Agent Orange, asbestos, and the chemical contamination at Love Canal. When I read this list, I developed serious doubts about the merits of investing further time in the book. After all, in discussing any of these issues, Simon had cited no more than two data sources apiece. This scanty list of sources was furthermore characterized by its nonscientific aspect. As for the issue of mercury in swordfish and tuna, he cited one unpublished document and one "personal correspondence" by the same author. Such is the evidence for "definitely disproven"?

As his writing wore on, Simon succumbed to circular reasoning and self-contradiction. For example, he made one claim that rising prices are the only reliable indicator of resource shortage, and another that timber supplies were not declining. And what were his explanations for the latter? "Perhaps the most important have been conservation efforts due to higher prices" (p. 160). Later, while arguing that there was no limit to the efficiency of engines, Simon noted that an early steam engine "operated at 1 percent efficiency" (p. 181), which of course entails a limit (100 percent) to the engine's efficiency. Perhaps the most flagrant contradiction was Simon's mantra that governmental regulation is the real problem underlying inefficient and insufficient resource allocation. Yet Simon habitually cited government regulations as prime examples of brainpower overcoming resource shortages. Nowhere is this self-contradiction more evident than in Simon's discussions of pollution in chapters 15–19.

At times, Simon's self-contradiction hinted at a dormant instinct that he just might have been wrong. For example, Simon's most notorious argument was that population growth is not something to fear for its ecological consequences but something to promote for its economic benefits. Yet he asserted, "To control fertility in response to the conditions facing them, people must be capable of rational, self-conscious forethought that affects the course of sexual passion, the kind of planning capability that animals apparently do not possess" (p. 344). In this incredible fit of irony, he stole the thunder of the very cloud he had saturated with cold water for most of his career.

Admittedly, it must be difficult to get through a 734-pager without having some contradiction seep in here or there. But in a very real sense, Simon's entire thesis was self-contradictory. In a nutshell, his thesis was that we didn't have to worry about ecological limits to economic growth because we would overcome such limits with brainpower. Why would such brainpower be employed? Because we would continually come up against ecological limits that would cause us to worry and therefore act! Not only is such a thesis self-contradictory, but it illustrates how some people promote the concern and put forth the effort needed to solve problems as the limits to growth are approached, while some watch and write about it, keeping their hands clean and their consumption up while they claim that there are no limits.

To be fair to Simon, I have naturally focused on the weaknesses of his *Ultimate Resource 2* to support my own argument. I acknowledge that Simon also provided some good arguments and a lengthy list of references that was not entirely devoid of scientific citations. And, despite the many weaknesses of his culminating effort, Simon's earlier writings should be accorded the respect they deserve. Simon was a clever, imaginative, and highly motivated man. But Simon did nothing to prove that limits to economic growth do not exist. Not surprisingly, Simon's arguments tended to lack the very common sense that he admonished his readers from employing. While Simon employed impressive quantities of time-series data, his less impressive theoretical underpinnings derived entirely from neoclassical growth theory. Ironically, the living icon of that theory, Robert Solow (1988: xvi), said in his 1987 Nobel lecture, "To believe as many American economists do that empirical economics begins and ends with time-series analysis, is to ignore a lot of valuable information that cannot be put into so convenient a form." Could Solow have been invoking common sense? Consider the fact that Solow referred to the "profound warning" he hung in his office, namely, "No amount of (apparent) statistical evidence will make a statement invulnerable to common sense" (1988:xxii).

The book you are reading, although it disagrees with one of Solow's conclusions pertaining to economic growth (that is, the endlessness thereof), is written in Solow's spirit of common sense.

# 5

# COPERNICUS, ARE YOU OUT THERE?

As the Emeritus Librarian of Congress Daniel J. Boorstin has documented, it is always difficult for a discoverer to gain the respect of those who presume a knowledge of the terrain. " 'Knowledge' was the barrier to knowledge," Boorstin (1983:344) said of the many medieval attempts to replace antiquated Greek anatomy. Leonardo da Vinci almost broke through the barrier, as a posthumous analysis of his writings revealed, but he was first and foremost an artist, so the many needed revisions had to wait for "real" students of anatomy like Vesalius. Likewise, it is always difficult for the chemist to gain the respect of the physics profession in matters of physics, or for the archeologist to gain the respect of geologists in matters of geology. Scholars in any discipline tend to presume that the only ones who can provide new insight to their field are the ones who have exclusively and exhaustively studied the field.

It is an order of magnitude more difficult for the discoverer, even one steeped in the discipline, when those doing the presuming are backed by powerful political interests and long-established cultural traditions. The explorer Columbus faced such difficulty in proclaiming that the Earth was round. The microbiologist Hooke faced it in proclaiming that living organisms consisted of cells. And Copernicus faced it in proclaiming a heliocentric planetary system.

As Kuhn pointed out in *Scientific Revolutions*, despite the lack of credibility afforded to discoverers from outside a discipline, they are precisely the ones with the best chance to discover. They do not suffer the tunnel vision of paradigm. They start with few assumptions, or in some cases with seemingly unrelated assumptions that turn out to be profoundly applicable. Aside from observers outside the discipline, younger practitioners from within the discipline, with less indoctrination, are more likely to make revolutionary discoveries.

In addition to pointing out *who* is likely to make a revolutionary discovery, Kuhn pointed out *when* a revolution is likely to occur. Scientific revolutions tend to occur in times of crisis. In science, a crisis occurs when data start to pile up that are inconsistent with a long-standing theory. For Ptolemy's cosmology, equants and epicycles were useful in explaining away the "anomalies" of planetary movements visible to the naked eye, but when telescopes came into focus in the seventeenth century, "anomaly" reached crisis proportions as it turned into reality. The Copernican revolution was enabled by the Ptolemaic crisis.

Perpetual economic growth has been the dominant theory for nearly a century, and talk about facing a crisis! First of all, growth in American gross national product has slowed in recent decades, straining the faith of many neoclassical economists. But this is nothing as earth-shaking as the proverbial telescope, because economies are known to cycle. (As I write, some mighty wild bull-riding is the main event on Wall Street, but the smell of bear is in the air.) Neoclassical economists fully expect the growth rate to wax and wane, but they also expect the economy to grow perpetually at *some* rate. More disturbing is the increasing amount of societal costs that get counted as contributing to economic growth. The millions wasted on the Exxon *Valdez* cleanup, and the billions wasted on tobacco-industried lung cancer are all dollars that contribute to the gross national product.

But where the crisis really lies is in the economically impacted environment, which is something growth economists have little understanding of. That is why the radical economists alluded to in previous chapters tend to come from the natural (physical and biological) sciences, from which they have delved into economic theory. The radicals also include economists with neoclassical training who have invested some time in the natural sciences. They have acknowledged the shortcomings of the social sciences, including their economic brethren, in formulating a more realistic model of economic growth. These radicals from the natural and social sciences have recognized the value of the economy of nature as a model for human economy. If there is a Copernican economics, perhaps it is to be found in their writings. Collectively, gradually, persistently, they have been developing a revolutionary model of economic growth called "ecological economics."

It might seem like a stretch to call this scientific development "revolutionary." For one thing, economics scarcely qualifies as a science. In fact, all of the social sciences have struggled to attain the scientific bearing of the natural sciences. This has to do with the difficulty of applying the scientific method (especially experimentation) to societies. If the scientific method is a crown, then physics has long been the jewel, biology the metal, and social sciences the interchangeable linings that get used once in awhile depending on the weather. A drastic change in economic thought would better be classified as a change in philosophy, a correction in logic, or an adaptation to current societal values—not a scientific revolution.

On the other hand, a thorough debunking of neoclassical economic growth theory would constitute a *real*, that is a *social*, revolution. Imagine what would happen if, from now on, every economics text in the nation, every economics professor interviewed, and every economist in government taught that we were approaching the limit to economic growth, with disastrous effects in the offing. How would you and the other 290 million Americans view that Wall Street report then? That exhortation to double the growth rate? That new factory opening near that new subdivision west of that new town? In other words, imagine what would happen if we the people had a *negative* view of economic growth, so that instead of valuing economic growth as highly as species conservation and property rights, we valued it as lowly as species extinction and property condemnation. What types of candidates would we elect? What types of cars would we drive? How much sway would the fat cats walk with? How many corporations would advertise their contributions to economic growth? Which industries would be subsidized? If you've thought about these questions, you've seen why this ecological economics movement is revolutionary in a *mother-of-revolutions* sense, if not in a scientific sense.

Of course, a revolution is defined not only by the magnitude of change in scientific perception or political power, but by the speed at which it occurs. Some of us hope for a revolutionary rate of change from neoclassical to ecological economics, because we are worried for the grandkids and are convinced that economic growth has become a threat to their welfare. That is why books like this are written as public tracts, and not as scientific monographs. The issue is not whether such books facilitate a scientific revolution, but whether they contribute to a real revolution, a bloodless but socially and politically powerful revolution that will knock economic growth off the pedestal of American ideology. For those who understandably are concerned with scientific credibility, the data sources and the common sense of such books may readily be assessed. (You won't find any "personal correspondence" citations in this book.) But to get on with it, it is time to take a tour of this revolutionary, ecological economics with its physical, biological, and social underpinnings.

Let's start with physics. In terms of transcending the field of economics, perhaps the most profound applications have been elaborated by Nicholas Georgescu-Roegen, a professor in the department of economics at Vanderbilt University. Trained as a statistician and mathematician at the Sorbonne, he also studied physics and, eventually, economics at Harvard under the prolific Joseph Schumpeter. So Georgescu-Roegen took his mathematical education, supplemented it with a knowledge of physics, and, familiarized but not indoctrinated with neoclassical theory, moved on to economics.

In the Distinguished Lecture Series at the University of Alabama, Georgescu-Roegen (1993:78) proposed that thermodynamics (defined as the branch of science concerned with the nature of heat and its conversion into other forms of energy) is really "a physics of economic value." He pointed to the first law of thermodynamics, which essentially states that matter can be neither created nor destroyed. Right away, this physical law implies an upper boundary to goods production, enforced by the amount of matter on Earth. Man did nothing to "produce" goods in a literal, thermodynamic sense.

Georgescu-Roegen proceeded to describe economic production from the perspective of the second law of thermodynamics, which states that in any closed system, from a test tube of ice to a planet and its atmosphere, things gradually become disordered. In the language of thermodynamics, entropy (disorder) continuously increases. To economics, the entropy law means that one produces a good (something ordered and directly useful) only by using energy to transform a raw material (something of lesser order and less directly useful). The energy is then contained in the ordered good, but has simultaneously been depleted from the good's surroundings. This means that an increase in utility somewhere comes only with a decrease in utility elsewhere. The resulting items of decreased order and therefore lesser utility to man are called byproducts, waste, or pollution. They pile up and get in the way, sometimes threatening man with their toxicity, while the useful items break down, get polluted, and gradually become sources of pollution themselves.

An example provided by Georgescu-Roegen is the refining of copper ore, a relatively disordered substance of little direct utility to man. Through the refining process, the highly ordered substance of solid copper is produced. However, the major step in the refining process (smelting) involves the loss of another highly ordered substance of direct utility (natural gas or coal). The byproducts of smelting include mining slag and atmospheric emissions, including greenhouse gases. A great many other physical and chemical exchanges are entailed from the ore body to the sheet of copper, but basically this sector of economic "production" is a trade of ordered goods and energy for copper.

Furthermore, Georgescu-Roegen (1993:80) pointed out that the trade results in a net loss for economic *potential*. In his terms, "The refining of copper ore causes a more than compensating increase in the entropy of the surroundings." In other words, the cumulative order and available energy of the goods and services going into the process is greater than that coming out. This too follows from the entropy law.

Although Georgescu-Roegen does not put it in these terms, we see that the issue of efficiency is afoot once again. We've all heard it said that nothing is perfectly efficient. Your automobile cannot use all of the energy contained in the gasoline that fuels it. Quite a bit escapes, not only in the chemical exhaust, but in heat radiating from the engine block itself. As Georgescu-Roegen (1993:80) put it, "In entropy terms, the cost of any biological or economic enterprise is always greater than the product. In entropy terms, any such activity necessarily results in a deficit." And that deficit means reduced economic capacity in the future. So more economic growth today translates to less economic growth tomorrow; and "every time we produce a Cadillac, we do it at the cost of decreasing the number of human lives tomorrow" (p. 85).

Now neoclassical economics has been criticized for its portrayal of the economic process as an isolated, circular affair. Stripped to the bone, it says that production leads to consumption, and consumption leads to production. This is a closed circle, so the neoclassical economist ought not audaciously ignore the entropy law and claim that order (and therefore value) within the circle will continually increase. But in an ironic twist, the neoclassical economist can turn the tables and point out that Earth, in fact, is not a closed system. In a geological, atmospheric sense, it essentially is closed, but in an energy sense, it is open to the rays of the sun, the source of all energy on earth except nuclear. Julian Simon, for one, turned precisely this table.

Yet beware the argument and keep turning the table. It is true that almost all non-nuclear energy on Earth comes from the sun, even hydroelectric and wind power (because the sun's energy sets into motion the Earth's atmosphere and hydrosphere in the process known as climate). As we have seen, some of the sun's energy is captured in the chloroplasts of green plants, the bottom line for all economies, human and nonhuman. Formed from fossilized plants, fossil fuels represent an ancient photosynthetic harvest. But it is not true that the sun represents some infinite source of energy. And I am not resorting to a premature announcement of the sun's death, the sun having a few billion years of hydrogen left. I am referring to the immediate concern of the sun's output while alive. Mathematically, we simply cannot use more energy than that received from the sun on a sustainable basis. We can only do so in the short term by tapping its prior achievements such as fossil fuels. And tap them we do, using 40 percent more fossil energy in the United States than the total amount of solar energy captured every year by our vegetation (Vitousek et al. 1986).

Admittedly, that is not the same as saying that we cannot tap more energy from the sun than we currently do. After all, much of the United States is paved over and lacks vegetation to capture sunlight. Perhaps with solar panels we could avail ourselves of massive quantities of energy.

To digress momentarily from this tour of ecological economics, let us consider an unconventional perspective on solar power. To do so we have to broach the scientifically and politically sensitive topic of global warming. The scientific merit of this book is in no way dependent on the existence of global warming, but it is worth mentioning that, when I wrote this portion of the book during October 1998, the National Climatic Data Center had just announced that the previous month was the warmest September on record. It was almost a full degree Fahrenheit above the previous record, and nearly four degrees Fahrenheit above the average. It was the ninth consecutive month to break the previous all-time record. Read it any way you like.

Global warming is a topic in which few of us have formal training. But just like much of economics is a matter of common sense, which we all share by definition, global warming has some traits that we can all grasp quite readily. First, we all know that warming means more heat, which is just a form of energy. We know that the sun is the major source of energy, and therefore heat, on Earth. We know that, currently, a major share of the sunlight reaching the Earth is reflected back into space. Now I'm no brain surgeon, but doesn't it stand to reason that, if we capture more of this energy for use on Earth, the temperature of our atmosphere will rise? In statistical jargon, the only doubt is whether or not the rise will be "significant." Well let's see . . . seems like the more that's captured, the more likely it is to be significant! So if neoclassical growth theory stakes a claim on perpetually increased solar capture, won't it succumb to the fact that the economy's participants are gonna fry?

And why shouldn't we expand this common sense to include economic growth as a whole, with or without a dependence on solar power? During the early stages of this manuscript, I was renting a room in a house. The landlord, who also lived in the house, was a bright fellow who worked as an insurance adjuster. He had taken business and economics courses in college, although he hadn't studied the natural sciences. One evening we were watching the national news, which featured a long segment about how the economy, though still growing, showed many signs of laboring. Doomsayers were predicting a downturn, maybe even all the way to a shrinking economy! Panic on Wall Street, sadness all about.

Next, they had an equally long segment on global warming. They provided some of the earlier data from the National Climatic Data Center, and I was surprised that they basically came out and said, "It's really happening, folks." But they said little about the causes. They showed factories spewing out pollutants, presumably alluding to the warming effect of greenhouse gases. To me it looked like a lot of those stacks were just pumping out steam, and I remembered a study that showed how warming due to waste heat emission exceeded global warming, at least within urban areas (Viterito 1991). I said to my landlord, "Look at all that heat coming out of there. Doesn't it seem like the economic activity they were rooting for in the last segment might be contributing to the warming, at least in those cities where they all seem to live?" The landlord thought for a minute and said, "Gee, I would have never thought about it like that. That's interesting. Yeah, I see what you mean." Common sense. Yet people who downplay the merits of common sense propose "orbiting giant mirrors that would reflect sunlight onto the night side of the Earth and thereby increase growing time" (see chapter 4).

But back to the radical pioneers in ecological economics. In the natural sciences, the major division is between the physical and biological. While Georgescu-Roegen was outlining the physical laws that limit economic growth, the ecologist Paul Ehrlich was outlining the biological. Not the Paul Ehrlich who won a Nobel Prize in 1908 for his discoveries in immunology, but the Paul Ehrlich who has received all kinds of other accolades for writing *The Population Bomb* in 1968. Ehrlich is a biology professor at Stanford University with a specialty in butterfly ecology, and prior to his venture into economics had mastered the calculus of animal population dynamics. He was one of the first, and surely the most notable, to apply the ecological concept of carrying capacity to human economies. Despite the academic rigor in which his findings are rooted, Ehrlich remains one of the champions of common sense in matters of ecology and economy by warning his peers to avoid the "rigor trap." "Plenty is known," Ehrlich (1994:39) says, "about the directions in which humanity should be moving to establish a 'sustainable' society."

Carrying capacity, or "K," is understood by biologists to mean the maximum population of a given species that an area can support without reducing its ability to support the same species in the future. Carrying capacity is determined by the availability of resources and by the species' consumptive habits. If you haven't witnessed it yourself, common sense will tell you that a certain forest can carry only a certain amount of deer. Forest conditions may change, at times becoming more favorable for deer and at other times less, so K may change over time. If one likes to flirt with the rigor trap, a good way to start is by averaging the K's over time to produce a long-term K. But with deer, the concept is fairly simple because at least the consumptive requirements remain fairly constant.

Animal populations at low levels reach their carrying capacity in two fundamentally distinctive fashions. One is called sigmoid growth because of the sigmoid (s-shaped) pattern it exhibits when graphed (see figure 1). In this fashion, the population increases rapidly while resources (like food and cover) are abundant. As

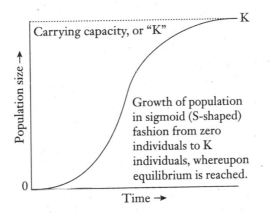

Figure 1. Population growth exhibited by
K-selected species

resources are used up, population regulation factors (like lower birth rates) come into play, and the rate of population growth slows. Eventually, as carrying capacity is reached, the growth rate tapers off to zero and the population reaches a stable level at K. Species that exhibit such population growth patterns are called "K-selected."

In the second fashion (figure 2), the population increases rapidly, as does the population growth rate (or "r"). Population regulation factors do not come into play until the population outstrips the resources available to support it, at which time the primary regulation factor is mortality. In other words, the population explodes past K, and then crashes to a low level. The resources may then be replenished to some extent, whereupon the population can start all over again. This is a boom-and-bust cycle, and species that exhibit such a pattern are called "r-selected." (This is essentially the pattern attributed to humans by the classical economist Thomas Malthus.)

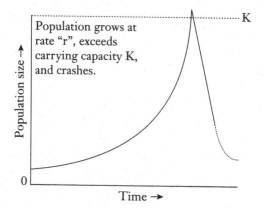

Figure 2. Population growth exhibited by an
r-selected species

Ehrlich recently summarized his application of the carrying capacity concept to economics. He distinguished between two kinds
of K for human beings. The first kind was biophysical K, or the
maximum number of people that can be supported at given levels
of technology. The second was social K, or the maximum number that can be supported at a given level of technology within a
given social organization, including patterns of consumption and
trade. Thus the social K would be higher "for a global society of
vegetarian saints than for a global society with the consumption
preferences of rich Americans" (1994:42). With this distinction,
Ehrlich acknowledges the difference between humans and deer;
humans have highly variable consumptive habits. Recognizing
that humans are motivated to exist at levels much higher than bare
subsistence, he deems only the social K as applicable to economic
discussion.

What Ehrlich is essentially doing here is applying the concept
of carrying capacity not only to the human population, but to the

human economy. In other words, the raw math of human numbers is only one part of the equation in determining the approach of the human economy to its carrying capacity. Ehrlich provides the equation, $I = P \times A \times T$, where I stands for impact—the impact of humans on their environment; P stands for population; A stands for affluence (or per capita consumption); and T stands for technological damage. None of these factors can be deemed secondary to the others. All else equal, an increase in any factor brings the human economy closer to carrying capacity. Rising levels of population and affluence simply increase the level of the human economy, thus bringing it closer to its carrying capacity in direct fashion. While a rising level of technology may increase economic efficiency, the impacts of such technology (like pollution) can lower the level of carrying capacity itself, thus "bringing" the economy closer to carrying capacity in a backwards fashion.

As a biologist, Ehrlich likes to focus on the impact of technology on ecological diversity. As natural ecosystems are liquidated by the technological implements of agriculture, mining, logging, industry, and urban development, the diversity of the land and its plant and animal communities is lost. In the process, economic values are lost, too. For example, wetlands are filters for human water supplies, spawning grounds for fish, and waterfowl production areas. They host a myriad of species that provide "ecological services" like carbon sequestration, nutrient recycling, pollination, and fertilization. When a wetland of highly complex hydrology and biology is drained, planted to corn, and sprayed with pesticides, the wild species native to the wetland are replaced by a monoculture designed to support a single, simplistic food chain —corn to humans (sometimes via beef cattle). The result? Exposed by large-scale tillage, the soil erodes. Without the sponge-like effect of the wetland, the area is prone to devastating floods. Without the continual decomposition of all kinds of organisms, the soil loses fertility and requires unsustainable, artificial fertilization. Without the myriad of natural insect predators, the crop is prone to devastation by insecticide-resistant pests. The one crop, often a genetically simplified one, is susceptible to disease epidemics. Freed from competition with native species, exotic weeds are a continual challenge. This scenario has played itself out from Maine to California, so of the 1,107 federally listed endangered species, 224 are endangered by agricultural activities (Czech and Krausman 2000). Similar scenarios have resulted from technology of all sorts.

Ehrlich (1994:43) calls the technological environment of economic growth an increasingly "weedy world," in which the carrying capacity for human economy actually declines. In other words, as technologically enabled economic growth proceeds, it does so at the expense of future economic capacity. This conclusion is strikingly similar to that reached by Georgescu-Roegen, which should come as no surprise. The economy of nature, whether described in physical or biological terms, is subject to the same natural laws.

The trained economists from ecological economics, having recognized the intersection of physical and biological theory in discussions of human economy, commonly refer to the "biophysical limits" to economic growth. Probably the most notable figure among them is Herman Daly, a professor of economics at the University of Maryland. Shortly after Georgescu-Roegen and Ehrlich had come upon the scene, Daly edited the landmark book, *Toward a Steady-State Economy* (1973). And here we come upon an alternative to economic growth. By a steady state economy, Daly meant an economy with a constant stock of physical wealth (capital) and a stable population, with minimal rates of "throughput." A minimal rate of capital throughput refers to low production and consumption, and a minimal rate of human throughput refers to low birth and death. What this amounts to is long-lived people, replenishment of resources as they are used, and low levels of pollution. But as Daly (1993:29) acknowledged, "The limits regarding what rates of depletion and pollution are tolerable must be supplied by ecology."

Daly was not the first economist to think in terms of a steady state. He noted that John Stuart Mill had spoken of the "stationary state" in 1857. Mill was best known for his ability to synthesize the philosophy of his fellow classical economists, and wrote at a time when great minds in all fields had a decent background in the sciences, natural and social. So Mill wrote, "It must always have been seen, more or less distinctly, by political economists, that the increase in wealth is not boundless: that at the end of what they term the progressive state lies the stationary state. . . . " Exhibiting an intuitive understanding of the principle of competitive exclusion, Mill continued:

It is not good for a man to be kept perforce at all times in the presence of his species. . . . Nor is there much satisfaction in contemplating the world with nothing left to the spontaneous activity of nature; with every rood of land brought into cultivation, which is capable of growing food for human beings; every flowery waste or natural pasture plowed up, all quadrupeds or birds which are not domesticated for man's use exterminated as his rivals for food, every hedgerow or superfluous tree rooted out, and scarcely a place left where a wild shrub or flower could grow without being eradicated as a weed in the name of improved agriculture. If the earth must lose that great portion of its pleasantness which it owes to things that the unlimited increase of wealth and population would extirpate from it, for the mere purpose of enabling it to support a larger, but not a happier or a better population, I sincerely hope, for the sake of posterity, that they will be content to be stationary, long before necessity compels them to it (from Daly 1993:27–28).

Mill did not view the stationary state as a dreadful prospect, either. In fact, he viewed it as an improvement, a state in which people could finally relax a bit and smell the roses. In a stationary state, he reasoned, people could substitute their striving for economic growth with a striving for cultural, moral, and social progress. Now *that's* substitution!

A slight digression is now required to clarify an issue of terminology. The term "steady state" is not the exclusive domain of ecological economics. Neoclassical economists use the term to describe the situation in which capital investment equals capital depreciation. Nevertheless, because the labor force grows and technology progresses, economic growth proceeds. Theoretically, population growth and technological progress may have steady rates, in which case neoclassical economists employ the phrase "steady state growth." We should not worry about this oxymoronic and esoteric rendering of "steady state" penetrating the American vernacular, however. The more intuitive "steady state economy," with its stable population and per capita consumption, stands a much better chance of that.

What Daly did, then, was help to resurrect and elaborate the classical wisdom that was lost to neoclassical economics. He and his fellow radicals from the economics profession are essential to hoisting this wisdom up onto the pedestal of the economics paradigm, because unlike the physicists and biologists, they understand the finer nuances of neoclassical argument. They know how to talk shop on economics topics from monetary policy to international trade, topics with implications for economic growth that evade most natural scientists. So it is not surprising that they have rooted out the *economic* sources of neoclassical weakness. The neoclassical growth model, they point out, recognizes just two factors of production. Before the Industrial Revolution got seriously rolling, classical models did the same, recognizing land and labor as the only two factors of production. Somewhere in the transition from classical to neoclassical economics, capital was added to the list, so then we had "land, labor, and capital." But neoclassical economists seem to have dropped land from the equation!

Care must be taken not to build a strawman here. At first, when I read about this in the ecological economics literature, I wondered if it was an exaggeration. After all, who could come to the crazy conclusion that capital and labor are sufficient to support an economy? So I investigated and, sure enough, the neoclassical theory of economic production recognized only labor and capital. However, land (and natural resources) was simply included as a subset of capital. So in a textbook entitled *Macroeconomics: A Neoclassical Introduction* the authors wrote that neoclassical economists consider the productivity of capital "as one of the technological facts of life, no more requiring an explanation by economists than the fact that putting one kernel of corn into the ground can return a whole ear of kernels at harvest time" (Miller and Upton 1974:21). The kernel of corn, whether placed in the soil by the scratching of fingernails or via a $70,000 row planter, was itself a unit of capital.

The problem is that the word "capital" has attained two distinct connotations in the vernacular, neither of which has to do with natural resources. The first is money. The second is man-made buildings, infrastructure, and equipment. Even for economists, it's pretty easy to forget that the original concept included land and natural resources. So in another textbook, entitled *Macroeconomics* and written fourteen years later, the authors note that "Many underdeveloped Third World nations . . . are stymied in their growth prospects because of a lack of productive labor or capital equipment or because their population is growing as fast as or faster than their output of real goods and services" (Ekelund and Tollison 1988:457). The factors of production have thus been reduced to labor and man-made capital. And this is not an isolated oversight but a common attitude. Moving from textbooks to the popular press, the president of the National Association of Manufacturers has asserted that the "long-term path for the economy is determined by the supply-side components of labor, the stock of physical capital (machinery and structures), and technological advance" (Jasinowski 1998:xxi). So to labor and human-made capital, technology or "human capital" is added to the factors of production. Carrying the concept of capital substitutability to an extreme, Robert Solow (1974:11) even suggested that, "The world can, in effect, get along without natural resources." Perhaps due to his aforementioned pursuit of common sense, however, Solow is said to have "since moderated his views on this subject" (Prugh et al. 1995:17).

In response to this tendency of neoclassical economists to forget about natural resources, and in response to the evolution of the term "capital," ecological economics has put a great deal of effort into developing the concept of "natural capital" and getting it recognized as an essential factor of economic production. Natural capital is a fancy way of saying natural resources. Trees, water, grass, petroleum, and fish are all natural capital. But using the term "natural capital" is important, because if neoclassical economists will acknowledge only labor and capital as the factors of production, then it is important to continually remind them that there are two major types of capital (man-made and natural), and that of the two, only natural capital is absolutely essential.

To understand the latter claim is a simple two-step process. First, one looks at the economy of nature, where the *only* type of capital is natural and where plenty of activity takes place. Prehistoric man experienced such an economy, and relatively recent tribal cultures came close, having little more man-made capital than a few hunting and farming implements. Second, one tries to envision an economy with people and machines, but no natural capital. What would the people eat? What would the machines produce? If you were around in the 1970s, pondering such questions might invoke the image of Charlton Heston kicking and screaming, "Soylent Green is people! Soylent Green is people!" (If you weren't around in the 1970s, Soylent Green was pressed out in wafer form, at night, in hidden factories.)

Furthermore, the concept of natural capital is superior to that of natural resources because neoclassical economists recognize capital as something from which valuable services flow. For example, ideas flow from human capital. Gadgets flow from man-made capital. And from natural capital, we have such flows as flood control, waste assimilation, nutrient recycling, soil formation, pollination, foods that nourish human minds, and raw materials for gadgets.

Another reason economists are so important to developing an ecological economics is that, being generally well versed in the social sciences, they readily note the negative impacts of economic growth not only on natural resource stocks and therefore indirectly on social welfare, but directly on social welfare. For example, what causes government to grow and get more intrusive? What causes congestion with its related stress and crime? What causes the displacement of the family farm? At bottom, population growth and resource consumption are the problems, while a steady state economy is the solution.

And while natural scientists have developed a solid body of theory for a limit to economic growth, they have not been as productive in developing alternatives. Relative to natural scientists, economists tend to be versed in social studies like political science, public administration, and sociology. Thus, they have envisioned social institutions that would serve a steady state economy.

The late Kenneth Boulding, professor of economics at the University of Michigan for two decades, proposed child licenses. (I was advised by reviewers to avoid this tabooed topic. However, I am neither condoning nor condemning the concept, but relating it in the spirit of exploration.) Each person would be endowed with a license to have 1.1 children, so that each couple would have a joint license for 2.2 children—the approximate number which, after child mortality and other population factors are taken into account, leads to a stable population. Couples wanting more children could purchase license quantum from couples wanting two or less. Those exceeding their licensed allotment would be fined. Couples who could not afford to raise more than two children would therefore be dissuaded from doing so, and the responsibility for preventing overpopulation (and too much economic activity) would be consciously borne by all. One of the fundamental conditions of a steady state economy (that is, a stable population) would be the result of a successful licensing system.

Child-bearing taxes are another possibility for moving toward a stable population. Such taxes sounds draconian, but they are essentially the same types of incentives—like tax breaks—that we now implement for *having* children, only in reverse.

Boulding was not obsessed with population growth. He covered all aspects of economic growth, and his book *Structure of a Modern Economy* helped to show how economies are integrated and do not therefore grow sector by sector, each independent of the other. In other words, he helped to show how an information economy was nothing but a regular economy at fruition. Well-schooled as he was in neoclassical economics, he nevertheless recognized the folly of perpetual growth. In solemn thought he spent his time, yet Boulding produced an occasional rhyme (in Rodes and Odell 1992:61):

> One principle that is an ecological upsetter
> Is that if anything is good, then more of it is better,
> And this misunderstanding sets us very, very wrong,
> For no relation in the world is linear for long.

Robert Costanza, the director of the Maryland International Institute for Ecological Economics and a professor at the University of Maryland, is one of the ecological economists who believes in market-based incentives to achieve ecological and economic sustainability. He begins with the assumption that the total stock of natural capital should not be lowered, because the flows of ecological services already appear insufficient, as evidenced by such disturbing trends as species endangerment, global warming, and ozone depletion. He argues that these trends are allowed to occur because natural capital is not accounted for in measurements of economic welfare like gross national product (GNP). He condones replacing GNP with the Index of Sustainable Economic Welfare (ISEW), which improves upon GNP by accounting for pollution and depletion of natural capital. While the price of a smokestack scrubber would contribute to GNP, it would be subtracted from ISEW. Seems like common sense.

Critic of common sense that he was, it was not surprising when Julian Simon (1996:231) said of the ISEW, "Regrettably, mainstream economists have not dignified this work with solid critique, to my knowledge. I confess that I cannot make head or tail of this writing." Then again, the only citation Simon provided when discussing the ISEW was a two-page article in a "News and Comment" section of *Science*.

To slow the depletion of natural capital, Costanza also recommends a natural capital depletion tax, which would focus on energy consumption. Petroleum and natural gas, especially, should be taxed heavily because they are nonrenewable resources. The injection of cash into the federal treasury would be compensated for by a decrease in the income tax. In addition to conserving resources, the general effect would be to redistribute wealth from industry and gas guzzlers to common folk.

One would court trouble by failing to acknowledge that, with respect to natural capital accounting, Costanza takes a page from the neoclassical book. Like their classical forebears, neoclassical economists place great faith (but not total faith since Keynes) in the market. And some of them have ventured forth into the subject of natural resources. They view things like natural resources depletion and pollution in terms of market failure, and therefore see solutions in fixing the market. For example, they generally support the privatization of public lands, in order to fulfill the free market assumption of private ownership of goods. Supposedly the national parks, for example, would be protected by the market, as long as they were really worth protecting. This school of thought, which is essentially the application of neoclassical economics to environmental affairs, is called "environmental economics," and it has been around since the 1960s, or even earlier if one includes the related efforts of "natural resource economics." In other words, environmental economics is a subset of neoclassical economics, and not to be confused with ecological economics. Therefore, some ecologists view Costanza's efforts as counterproductive, because they seemingly play into the precepts of neoclassical economics.

When Costanza and twelve co-authors had the audacity to value the world's ecosystem services (such as pollination and decomposition) at approximately $33 trillion per year in a 1997 edition of *Nature*, there was a big to-do about it on the Internet, one that continues today. Many ecological economists point out, and rightly so, that the value of nature cannot be described in monetary terms. But for the neoclassical economists who remain convinced that everything can be valued monetarily, perhaps these valuation exercises will help bring attention to the enormous values that are lost as economic "growth" liquidates natural capital.

Costanza (1994:400) has promoted other devices conducive to a steady state economy, including the "precautionary polluter pays principle" and a system of ecological tariffs. These devices, which have been floating around in the literature for at least twenty years, are geared toward making industries and nations ecologically accountable for their economic actions.

Then there is Warren A. Johnson, who has proposed the concept of a guaranteed income, whereby the federal government would invest in America's future by paying everyone an annual stipend. The amount would be low enough to be fiscally feasible, but high enough to encourage many folks to work less hours, or to divert their energy to charitable causes. In other words, they would contribute less to economic production, and economic growth would be slowed. (Something about this scheme seems awry, like getting something for nothing. But maybe there is something to it; our federal government has been doing it on a small scale for decades with its welfare programs.)

Amongst these pioneers of political economy, there are some who focus on the sociology of an ecological economics. Stephen Viederman, an economist with the Jessie Smith Noyes Foundation in New York, proposes outright political activism in order to get for ecological economics its due recognition. He wants the International Society for Ecological Economics (which numbers about 1,200 members) to maintain a contingent that refines a vision of a sustainable society, and places that vision in front of the eyes of our political leaders. Furthermore, he wants that vision to go beyond the issue of carrying capacity and to incorporate human dignity, something else the neoclassical pursuit of wealth tends to ignore. For Viederman (1994:472), "A sustainable society is one that ensures the health and vitality of human life and culture and of nature's capital, for present and future generations. Such a society acts to stop the activities that serve to destroy human life and culture and nature's capital, and to encourage those activities that serve to conserve what exists, restore what has been damaged, and prevent future harm." Viederman acknowledges the political stability required to achieve this vision, and points out that, without equity, there is no stability. So he proposes that equity become a primary concern of ecological economics, as it was with classical and Marxist economists. This proposal is strongly supported by the recently elected president of the International Society for Ecological Economics, Richard Norgaard (who we earlier found uprooting Julian Simon's fallacious theory of price as an indicator of scarcity).

Viederman also laments the social short-shrifting of pioneering scholars. He encourages ecological economists to resist the scientific publication race and to participate in the policy process, or at least publish in public forums. This book is written in the spirit of Viederman's exhortation.

Another ecological economist at the forefront of defining sustainability is John Gowdy, a professor at Rensselaer Polytechnic Institute in New York—one of the few American institutions with a graduate degree in ecological economics. Gowdy has helped to develop the distinction between "strong" and "weak" sustainability. His description of strong sustainability is generally consistent with Viederman's vision and certainly with Daly's steady state economy (Gowdy 2000). But Gowdy has thoroughly analyzed the neoclassical version of sustainability and found it weak indeed. Neoclassical economists calculate sustainability with a formula that, while not mind-boggling, doesn't quite belong in a book like this. The key assumptions are that sustainability is indicated by a nondeclining stock of capital, and that natural capital may be substituted for by manufactured substitutes or even cash.

Gowdy has applied the neoclassical formula to the Pacific Island of Nauru, where several thousand Nauruans occupy a narrow coastal strip and live off the interest of a billion-dollar trust fund. The money came from a massive inland phosphate deposit. The phosphate was mined and the landscape rendered uninhabitable. Having liquidated their inland natural capital, the Nauruans' subsistence is a matter of purchasing goods, including drinking water, on the international market to supplement their modest coastal fishery. Yet according to the neoclassical calculation of sustainability, Nauru's score of 33 identifies its economy as one of the most sustainable on earth (Gowdy and McDaniel 1999)!

Such an outcome redounds to the discredit of neoclassical assumptions. It fails to highlight the fact that the Nauruans won't have a pot to pee in if the trust fund is mismanaged or corrupted. Or that, if all nations sell their landscapes to keep *their* trust funds growing, the Nauruans won't have anyone to purchase food from. Or that the Nauruans will be stuck on a mined-out moonscape if global warming causes the sea to take over their coastline. The new face of Nauru must be very scary to the Nauruans who stop to think about it. Now imagine the fate of your grandkids being linked to the neoclassical concept of sustainability. Ascribing the term "weak" to this version of sustainability is generous indeed; "fake sustainability" or just plain unsustainability seem more accurate.

Scarily, such an inane concept of sustainability may be less exceptional than representative of neoclassical models. As one fellow put it,

> Page after page of professional economic journals are filled with mathematical formulas leading the reader from sets of more or less plausible but entirely arbitrary assumptions to precisely stated but irrelevant theoretical conclusions (from Hodgson 1996:5).

And who was the fellow who put it this way? Wassily Leontief, himself a Nobel Laureate in economics!

To summarize, ecological economics has developed a body of theory that recognizes physical and biological limits to economic growth. Viewing the environmental degradation caused by economic growth as an academic crisis for economics and a social crisis for posterity, ecological economics has sought alternatives to the goal of economic growth. Invoking some of the wisdom of classical economists, ecological economics recognizes the necessity and desirability of a steady state economy. Finally, ecological economics has begun to develop a body of policy tools that would help in attaining a steady state economy. Ecological economics is clearly not the "normal science" that Kuhn talked about. By parting with the status quo in the midst of crisis, ecological economics is a post-normal, revolutionary economics.

This chapter is but a whirlwind tour of ecological economics and does little justice to the many physicists, biologists, and radical economists that have contributed profoundly to this revolutionary movement. For those interested in a broader account, *A Survey of Ecological Economics* (Krishnan et al. 1995) is a collection of nearly a hundred condensed, classic papers in the field. For those who have found even the current chapter a test of their patience for detail, a better source would be *Natural Capital and Human Economic Survival* (Prugh et al. 1995), an effort by the International Society for Ecological Economics to synthesize the work of its practitioners in layman's terms.

As for the current effort, I think we have come far. We have been reminded of just how cherished economic growth is to the American public. We have explored the meaning of economic growth, and documented some of the negative results of increased production and consumption. We have found the neoclassical economic growth theory misguiding, but have not been surprised at its dominance because we have noted the powerful political and corporate interests that are served by the ideal of economic growth. We have summarized a new economic paradigm, a revolutionary worldview called ecological economics, from which we see that economic growth has become more a problem than a solution. Now it is time to consider what may be done to translate this revolutionary worldview into a steady state economy.

PART TWO

# STOPPING THE TRAIN

Social structure changes, develops, adapts itself to an altered situation, only through a change in the habits of thought of the several classes of the community; or in the last analysis, through a change in the habits of thought of the individuals which make up the community. The evolution of society is substantially a process of mental adaptation on the part of individuals under stress of circumstances which will no longer tolerate habits of thought formed under and conforming to a different set of circumstances in the past.

> THORSTEIN VEBLEN,
> *The Theory of the Leisure Class,*
> 1899

Growth chestnuts have to be placed on the unyielding anvil of biophysical realities and then crushed with the hammer of moral argument.

> HERMAN DALY,
> "Introduction to Essays Toward
> a Steady-State Economy," 1993

# THE STEADY STATE REVOLUTION
*Precepts and Terminology*

6

An old adage states that democracy is the recurrent suspicion that more than half of the people are right more than half of the time. We live in the world's model democracy—a fact for which to be supremely grateful—and for many of us, majority rule is indeed synonymous with democracy. However, majority rule has long been recognized by philosophers and historians as a dangerous principle that threatens the bigger picture of democracy, including equality, freedom of information, and public participation. This threat is called the tyranny of the majority. When misled, ignorant, or frenzied, the masses can wreak havoc. And yet, would we rather have a king, a dictator, or an aristocracy? The authors of the Constitution did the best that could be done by institutionalizing a system of checks and balances and the principle of representation. The Senate, for example, with its six-year terms, is supposed to have a cool head partially for the purposes of resisting short-term, poorly thought-out frenzies of public opinion.

But even the Constitution's elaborate system of governance

can't beat entropy. Nothing is free, and a democracy is ultimately dependent on an intelligent, caring, and participating majority for its success. Problems are solved only when such a majority develops a perspective conducive to the solution. Usually the perspective covers the problematic institution itself, and the primary institutional actors. For example, when the majority of Americans perceived slavery as an unjust institution, and perceived slaveowners as the unjust practitioners thereof, slavery was abolished. Some slaveowners resisted, but they eventually petered out because they were ostracized. Even prior to abolishment, as the public's opinion of slaveowning turned negative, the injustices of slavery were lessened because the behavior of slaveowners changed with the norms. The problem of child labor was solved in a similar manner. Advanced, long-enduring institutions have been uprooted in relatively short order when they and their perpetrators became reprehensible to the majority.

Since the founding of the nation, the American majority has held economic growth in high esteem, and the majority has not been failed by democracy. The economy went through a start-up stage and then took off in the rocket's red glare. It grew up to be big and strong; by 1913 it was the most productive in the world —in 1922 alone gross national product rose 18 percent—by 1989 its volume was 450 times that of the 1820 version. It grew not only in aggregate but in per capita terms; by 1900 the average income was about three times its 1800 counterpart, and by 1990 the average American's consumption expenditure was about four times the 1900 level (Madrick 1995). But somewhere along the line a threshold was crossed. Thereafter, Americans didn't become any happier with all the extra consumption. The transition appears to have taken place somewhere between 1955 and 1980 (Schor 1991, Frank 1999).

Now the economy bloats at a rate of about 2.5 percent per year —5 percent in particularly threatening years. If it is not to jeopardize the lives of the grandkids, its growth must taper off at or below carrying capacity in K-selected fashion (see chapter 5). This will require nothing less than a revolution, a social revolution to match the academic revolution of ecological economics. The total revolutionary package may be called the steady state revolution.

The steady state revolution will be nothing like, for example, a Marxist revolution. Marx was convinced on theoretical grounds that capitalism was doomed, that socialism was the next stage, and that the economic evolution of humans would culminate in communism. Personally, he was all for such a development. Politically, therefore, he called upon the working masses to revolt. The bourgeoisie would not relinquish its undeserved wealth without a fight; might as well fight it out right away and shorten the term of oppression.

The call for the steady state revolution bears no resemblance to Marx's, in the sense that its aim is not communism or any other replacement of a prudently managed capitalist democracy. And there is no call here for a forcible overthrow of anything. Americans black and white have proven a great deal about the effectiveness of nonviolent revolution. So have others all over the world. As Brown (1995:119) pointed out in *Models in Political Economy*, "Most revolutionary social changes have involved very little violence."

On the other hand, the call for a steady state economy is far more urgent than Marx's. Unlike his evolutionary perspective of communism, there is no reason to believe that a steady state economy is preordained. And this is worrisome, because as Brown (1995:119) also noted, "It is the social breakdown that follows a failure to change that engenders violence." Americans are exhibiting some highly r-selective traits, portending a failure to change that could culminate in violence. Cornell professor Robert Frank (1999) pointed out that luxury spending in the United States is growing more than four times as rapidly as spending overall. Luxury autos, mansions and second mansions, vast lots, huge yachts, gawdy home appliances, cosmetic procedures, ultrapremium wines—all are being consumed at unprecedented rates. The ridiculous magazine *Cigar Aficionado* had more than 400,000 paid subscribers in 1996, and subscriptions were increasing rapidly.

Worst of all, it is not just the super-rich accounting for such waste. For every mansion on a vast lot, there are hundreds or thousands of "McMansions" on large lots. While the super-rich buys a $30 million yacht, the plain-old-rich buys the $130,000 "bionic dolphin" (a one-person watercraft). For every million-dollar "Diamond Dream Bra," thousands of hundred-dollar bras are purchased. These incredible figures have been well documented by Frank (1999:37), who sensed a "growing social tolerance of acquisitiveness and greed."

While the super-rich are spending embarrassing amounts, anybody with the means seems to be following suit. In fact, all the way down the line we Americans seem to have a problem. We do it on credit, if necessary. By 1986, total spending in the United States came to 104 percent of GNP. How could that be? We borrowed $157 billion from foreign banks (Hamrin 1988). By 1988, the bunch of us spent $313 billion on leisure travel and over $200 billion on gambling (Paepke 1993). The throwaway nature of our consumerism is legendary; we drink more soda pop than water! A lot of the "consumption" is actually waste; we annually dump the equivalent of more than 21 million shopping bags full of food into landfills. Researchers from the State University of New York at Syracuse calculated that

> an American born in the 1990's would produce in a lifetime about one million kilograms of atmospheric wastes, ten million kilograms of liquid wastes, and one million kilograms of solid wastes. In addition, an American will consume 700 thousand kilograms of minerals, and 24 billion BTU's of energy, which is equivalent to 4 thousand barrels of oil. In a lifetime, an average American will eat 25 thousand kilograms of major plant foods and 28 thousand kilograms of animal products, provided in part by slaughtering two thousand animals (Hall et al. 1994:509–510).

These physical features are difficult to put into perspective, but there are telling psychological signs as well. For example, the fastest growing spectator sport in America is stock car racing; over 150 million Americans tuned in to watch at least one race in 1997. Some stock car races, like the Daytona 500, have attained prime-time TV coverage. What does this tell us about the American conservation ethic? How will the grandkids look back upon this folly? After all, racing amounts to intensive petrol consumption for exceedingly ephemeral gratification.

Perhaps these tendencies are related to the survey mentioned in chapter 1 that found that 63 percent of Americans agreed there were no limits to economic growth. As outlined in part 1, they have learned their neoclassical growth lessons well, either literally in the classroom or vicariously through the evening news.

It is very difficult to consider such aspects of American culture and conclude that we have a sustainable future. If Americans are indeed r-selected, the economy will stop growing all right, but not by reaching a steady plateau upon which to rest. It will stop growing in Malthusian fashion, with blight and despair in the offing as it crumbles amidst a wasted environment. While Marx's theoretical evolution was inexorably toward the good, and could be hastened via revolution, the real-world evolution is clearly toward the bad, and is hastened by the status quo!

In the world's model democracy, the steady state revolution must be a revolution in public opinion, a process by which the virtually ubiquitous cherishing of economic growth is transformed into an equally ubiquitous castigation of economic growth. This type of revolution is more social than political. It will not restructure the political system, but will replace the society of politicians with one of a different mind, with vastly different implications for the traditional beneficiaries of public policy. Majority opinion will be amenable to a steady state economy, and it will have to be sincere, explicit, and long term. Sincere means that people will act upon their convictions. Explicit means that the goal will be expressed in terms that cannot be misinterpreted by politicians who are supposed to represent the people. Long term means for the remainder of American existence, assuming that God declines to rewrite the biophysical laws.

Does the castigation of economic growth make the steady state revolution a moral affair? Only to the extent that the current cherishing of economic growth is a moral affair, and only to the extent that conserving the grandkids' inheritance is considered a moral issue. One could also classify it as an issue of economic sustainability, public health, or intergenerational justice. Each of these are put at risk by economic growth. Those with a vested interest in economic growth will probably build a strawman of the steady state revolution, portraying it as an emotionally driven attempt to enforce one set of morals on the rest of society. Such a portrayal will be a transparent attempt to buy time for economic growth and the attendant profits for some, and its transparency will increase as the economy congests and the environment degrades. In a concurrently increasing fashion, the steady state revolution will be seen by objective observers as a logical attempt to debunk a harmful myth that has been perpetuated by a cadre of professionals who serve (more or less wittingly) powerful economic interests.

Meanwhile, if the grandkids' prospects are an emotional issue for some, they surely cannot help it. Although one may claim on political grounds that such folks are driven by emotions, another may claim on scientific grounds that such emotions comprise an evolved survival instinct (Wilson 1998). The goal of the steady state revolution is to establish a steady state economy for the purpose of providing the grandkids (and their grandkids as well) a well-endowed natural environment conducive to health, happiness, and their own economic opportunities. The motives of such a goal should require little analysis. To the extent that the supporter of this goal may be portrayed as a bleeding heart, the opponent of this goal may be portrayed as a misanthropic deviant.

Although there is no reason to believe that this revolution in public opinion is preordained, there are reasons to be hopeful. Most importantly, people truly care about their grandkids, and even about their grandkids' grandkids. Couple this with our generally increasing aversion to risk, as documented by C. Owen Paepke in *The Evolution of Progress*, and we have to conclude that our wastefulness is less a matter of greed than ignorance. Our majority, misled by neoclassical economics and its corporate backers, is simply unaware of the magnitude of risks imposed by economic growth upon the grandkids. But the truth can be denied for only so long. The signs of economic growth gone awry are abundant: congestion, endangered species, and water shortages, for starters. All it will take is for more people to interpret such signs as the effect of economic growth, and not of other scapegoat phenomena. Ecological economics will be there to do the interpreting, and common sense will do the rest.

In thinking about a steady state revolution in public opinion, it will be useful to clarify a few terms. Words are incredibly important devices. Not words per se, but the connotations they produce, the baggage they carry, and the actions they invoke. A philosopher once remarked that there is no greater impediment to the advancement of knowledge than the ambiguity of words. Maybe, unless it is the *unambiguity* of words that are used in the wrong context. Take growth, for instance. Growth is not at all ambiguous. It means to increase, get larger, expand, blossom. It's what babies, puppies, and kittens do. For many people, the fondest memories are of childhood or adolescent growth. Knowledge grows, bank accounts grow, confidence grows. Good things grow, and when they don't grow, it is bad. To not grow generally means to shrink, shrivel, dwindle, wither.

When the term "economic growth" is used, people are predisposed toward a positive reaction. Now this might be a minor point if the term was used as often as "pumpernickel" or "molecular evolution." But the term economic growth is heard virtually every day by those who watch the news or read the newspapers. If you get through a day without hearing it, don't worry, it will catch up to you. Remember the Kemp quote from the 1996 vice presidential debate? That was far from the only mention of economic growth. Twenty-two topics were debated, only three of which pertained directly to the economy. Nevertheless, Kemp interjected calls for faster economic growth in thirteen of the topical categories.

True, there are many among us who have seen the phenomenon of growth run amuck. In individuals, we've seen cancer and obesity. In societies, we've seen fads and fascism. In nature, we've seen invasions and infestations. Still, we generally don't think of such phenomena in terms of growth, even growth gone awry. We think of them as diseases, disasters, or mistakes. Cancer, for example, is not referred to as growth, but simply as cancer. When it happens, it is the withering aftermath that is despised, not the preceding growth.

Furthermore, *economic* growth is a particular manifestation of growth that we have been conditioned to appreciate, cheer, and serve. After all, economic growth was, during most of its history, a wonderful thing for Americans. Of course, let us not forget the Native Americans, for whom the new American economy was a cultural death knell. But for the new Americans, for whom carrying capacity was a far-off ceiling, economic growth did mean better food, clothing, housing, and education. Understandably, the term economic growth could for many years engender happy, encouraging thoughts. That much is beyond our control.

Perhaps, then, we should find a replacement phrase with an equally powerful, but negative, connotation. Herman Daly once referred to "economic swelling"; I suspect "bloating" is more conducive to a paradigm shift. Swelling connotes an uncomfortable condition, one that usually goes away on its own, and it creates no real sense of alarm. With bloating, if you don't do something about it, the outcome is positively repugnant. For educated Americans who have come to recognize economic growth as a major problem, step number one in the steady state revolution is simple. Let's stop calling a major problem, perhaps the ultimate problem, something that has such a proud, positive connotation. That just invites the continued pulling of wool over eyes. Let's call it economic bloating.

A bloating economy, as with any economy, consists of households and firms, each of which are comprised of individuals. So an economy consists of individuals, some of whom are more responsible than others for economic bloating. This class of individuals is characterized by excessive consumption. The consumption is usually manifest in personal belongings, like cavernous homes, gas-guzzling cars, and yachts. Family members are responsible for such consumption. The consumption can be corporate too, like palatial headquarters, executive resorts, and private jet fleets. Boards of directors and chief executives are responsible for this type of consumption. Such family and corporate individuals are termed "wealthy," but "wealth" is another word to be wary of. It is often couched in meritorious terms, as in "healthy, wealthy, and wise." It is synonymous with "plenty," but while the plentiful object is usually money or valuable goods, one may also have a "wealth of knowledge" or a "wealth of friends." Because wealth, like growth, has such positive connotations, it behooves us to adopt a more representative term for those contributing disproportionately to economic bloating.

The term "bloated class" would be a bit unsophisticated for academics, and might therefore not be taken seriously. "Bourgeoisie" is too cliché and carries the big bag of communism. Perhaps the term "liquidating class" will do. This term has just enough sophistication to sound intellectually legitimate, but not enough to knock it out of American vernacular. Most importantly, it accurately reflects the problematic aspect of economic bloating. While the bourgeoisie was identified with the heartless oppression of the working class, the liquidating class is identified with the wanton destruction of the grandkids' natural environment. The liquidating class liquidates natural capital for the purposes of its own excess.

Of course, everyone liquidates to some extent. But just like the wealthy class was identified for having way *more* money than the other classes, the liquidating class liquidates way *more* of the environment. Some people live in bona fide mansions and own vacation homes. These folks liquidate via residence. Some drive Cadillacs on weekdays and Ferraris on weekends. These folks liquidate via transportation. Some accumulate expensive household items that sit there and do nothing (like the collector on the news this morning who spent $22,000 on some Mickey Mouse paraphernalia). These folks liquidate by collecting. Some people watch their big screen TVs from their thousand-dollar recliners; they liquidate via luxury. Some wear expensive fur coats and huge diamond rings; they liquidate by adorning themselves. Some live on porterhouse steaks and caviar; they liquidate with their stomachs.

Some pay hundreds a month on massages and hairdos; they liquidate by pampering themselves.

Although one must have a large quantity of money or assets to belong to the liquidating class, moneyed folks do not necessarily belong to the liquidating class. Once in awhile someone wins a million-dollar lottery and keeps the same small house, the same small car, and the same blue collar job. The money is saved or dispersed among family members, with large quantities given to charity. Such a person is clearly not a liquidator. The liquidating class is characterized by high levels of *wasteful* consumption, which amounts to the frivolous liquidation of the natural environment.

As with the term "wealthy class," the relativity of the term "liquidating class" causes some problems. If you're penniless, no one would call you a "liquidator." If you're Microsoft's Bill Gates, who built a $40 million house (complete with video walls and private trout stream), you're a liquidator in everyone's book. Even if you're only like Gates's counterpart at Oracle, Lawrence Ellison (whose Japanese-style *daimyo* house has a carp pool and a teahouse), you're still an obvious liquidator. The closer you get to this type of consumption, the more likely you are to be classified as a liquidator.

For the purposes of the steady state revolution in public opinion, let us consider the top one percent of people, in terms of personal consumption expenditure, to comprise the liquidating class. (We understand from the start that certain folks in this category are exempt, like devoted philanthropists.) Personal consumption expenditures—not including house purchases—account for almost 70 percent of gross domestic product (Stein and Foss 1995), and the proportion has been steadily rising since 1950. Personal consumption expenditures therefore comprise the primary source of economic bloating, and a source that is clearly amenable to modification via public opinion revolution. I will explain my selection of the one percent criterion, and the ease with which it may be applied, in chapter 7.

Because we have identified a particular class based on its tendency to liquidate exorbitant amounts of natural capital, we need a term that describes the people who conserve natural capital. These are the people whose consumptive behavior is conducive to a steady state economy. Many characteristics of this behavior come to mind: responsible, sustainable, modest, charitable, prudent. Of course, we can get carried away with attribution. Just as liquidators may not be aware of the consequences of their liquidating behavior, wealthy nonliquidators might merely be misers. So it would be misleading to call nonliquidators, for example, the "conscientious class." The term "sustainable class" would certainly be appropriate, because this class, conscientiously or not, offers our grandkids the hope of a sustainable future. But sustainable is a rather passive and dull term.

Perhaps the term "steady state class" will do. It would be identified readily with the class of people whose behavior is conducive to a steady state economy. Members of the steady state class, or "steady staters," would be known for their conservation, thrift, and (at least in conscientious cases) ethics. For the purposes of the steady state revolution in public opinion, let us consider the bottom 80 percent of people, in terms of personal consumption expenditure, to comprise the steady state class. I will explain the selection and application of the 80 percent criterion in chapter 8.

Finally, we need a term for those residing in the intermediate 19 percent of personal consumption expenditures. These folks vary tremendously in their liquidating habits, with a dubious effect on economic bloating. The term "amorphic class," encompassing as it were the "amorphs," will serve to capture the many and malleable consumption patterns displayed therein. Such patterns will be explored in chapter 9.

# RELATIONS WITH THE
# LIQUIDATING CLASS

If economic bloating is to be halted, the majority will have to develop a particular perspective of the liquidating class in the same manner that majorities developed perspectives of oppressive kings, slaveowners, or robber barons. Depending on the knowledge level of the liquidator, there basically are two appropriate steady state perspectives, each of which will be discussed, and neither of which are very congratulatory. As a forenote, however, this element of the steady state revolution is not revolutionary unto itself. Even while economic growth was good for society, the liquidating class was looked upon with some disdain. In 1913 the English poet Percy Bysshe Shelley observed, "The odious and disgusting aristocracy of wealth is built upon the ruins of all that is good in chivalry or republicanism; and luxury is the forerunner of a barbarism scarcely capable of cure." A similar if less caustic portrayal befell the landowners of David Ricardo's model, in which the workers and even the capitalists toiled while the wealthy landowners sat there and took advantage of the increasing land and food prices caused by population growth. And of course there was Marx, champion of the working class. He took the word "bourgeoisie" and made it infamous along with the class it described. Most important was Thorstein Veblen, whose *Theory of the Leisure Class* (1899) provides us with a good perspective of the liquidators, especially the unwitting ones.

Veblen is one of those academic legends who has taken on a posthumous life quite independent of the actual. Veblen wrote in a complicated and cryptic style, so a great many positions and points are attributed to Veblen with no firsthand knowledge of what the man actually wrote, and with little understanding of the actual meaning. As John Kenneth Galbraith pointed out in his 1973 preface to *Theory of the Leisure Class*, Veblen employed an "exceedingly perverse use of meaning." Per Galbraith's example, when Veblen used the term "waste," he didn't use it in its normal, deprecating sense. Instead, he used it to indicate esteem; only the esteemed wealthy could afford to waste.

But not only was the term "waste" bastardized, the "esteem" it represented was ludicrous. Veblen was presenting a cynical, castigating caricature of the snobby rich. Especially in the context of the Gilded Age, he couldn't come out and openly blast them without appearing spiteful or biased—recall the influence of wealth in academia (from which Veblen derived his livelihood). So he veiled his caricature in scientific argumentation. He used a knowledge of anthropology to compare the behavior of the wealthy to that of barbaric cultures, and he did it in a detached fashion that many interpreted as economic anthropology rather than sarcasm. No one acquainted with the enigmatic Veblen could tell how serious he was; we have little chance a century later.

To the extent that *Theory of the Leisure Class* jests, perhaps the last laugh is on Veblen (who might plausibly laugh along). There is no way of telling precisely how intentional it was, but Veblen's caricature dovetails quite well with *evolutionary* anthropology. Others have noted the factual, anthropological weaknesses— these exist and are not important here—but *Theory of the Leisure Class* provides a link between Charles Darwin's theory of evolution and Abraham Maslow's hierarchy of needs, a link that may be essential for understanding the behavior of the liquidating class. Before we continue with Veblen then, we need to briefly recount the pertinent works of Darwin and Maslow.

Darwin presented his theory of evolution in *Origin of Species*, published in 1859. The theory was based on the process of natural selection, or "survival of the fittest," in which various characteristics increase an animal's likelihood of survival and reproduction. The traits that increased its fitness—strength, for example —were likely to be selected for by nature, as the weak ones would be weeded out by predators, diseases, and competition with their own kind. The evolution of species would be facilitated by a mechanism that allowed traits to be passed on from one generation to the next. The later discovery of genetic inheritance and DNA provided the mechanism, and today the evidence for evolution via natural selection is practically incontrovertible.

The history of life as traced out by paleontologists, on the other hand, is quite controversial. I knew a fundamentalist who reconciled the fossil record with evolution by positing, "God created Adam as a mature man with mature bones. Why would God create a world without a mature fossil record?" Not a bad question, but we don't need the answer to address the motives of the liquidators.

Meanwhile, Abraham Maslow and his followers have been

called the "third force" in behavioral science (with Sigmund Freud and John Watson being the first and second, respectively). Maslow was a psychologist who was probably well versed in Veblen and Darwin. Maslow's hierarchy of needs, published in 1943, is one of the most enduring twentieth-century psychological theories. In a nutshell, Maslow said that people are motivated by the needs for nutrition, safety, love and affection (physical and psychological), self-esteem, and self-actualization, in that order. As one level of need is fulfilled, we move on to the next. Meanwhile, self-esteem is largely a function of what others think. So when the three most basic needs are met, we start focusing on impressing others, often with material wealth. Many of us, perhaps most, never make it to the level of self-actualization.

Supplement Darwin's evolution with Maslow's hierarchy, and you can explain much of the behavior on earth, human and non. Comparing the behavior of humans and nonhumans is even more enlightening. Just as the material economy of nature holds lessons for the *scale* of human economy, the social economy of nature holds lessons for the *sociology* of human economy.

In the economy of nature, elk display their antlers, peacocks display their tailfeathers, and sunfish display their gills. Not just figuratively, but literally. Antlers, tailfeathers, and gills demonstrate health, vigor, and dominance. They demonstrate the consumption of large quantities of high-quality food, the animal version of wealth. Accumulated wealth means longer antlers and brighter colors, and more vigorous display thereof.

Earlier in my career I spent hundreds of hours surveying elk in Idaho, Washington, and the San Carlos Apache Reservation in Arizona. The biggest elk in the world come from San Carlos, partly because we managed for a high ratio of males to females;

70 bulls for every 100 cows. This resulted in a mature age structure, where it was common to have twelve- and thirteen-year-old bulls running around. A twelve-year-old bull at San Carlos may have antlers nearly five feet long, with eight formidable tines on each side, the longest of which may exceed two feet. The bull himself may weigh 700 pounds. During the breeding season or "rut," his neck will be swollen and he will spend much of his time herding females and displaying himself. He will position himself sideways so the surface area of his antlers will be maximized for the intended audience, stretching his swollen neck out and up, antlers sweeping up and back in a great arc that may reach nearly to his rump. At full extension, nose lifted to the open sky and lips pulled back, he will emit a primordial wail that would make the hairs of the noninitiated jump right out of their roots. It starts out low in the lungs, almost imperceptibly, then builds in volume, octave, and urgency until you are, to understate it, thoroughly impressed. "Bugling," hunters so insufficiently call it (although the tilt of the snout is aptly described).

The methods of display, of course, are greatly multiplied for humans, who have an economic existence that extends far beyond their persons. Much farther than, for example, the bear's cave or the sparrow's nest, neither of which are employed at all for display. People display with homes and gardens, cars and boats, and even via Veblen's "conspicuous leisure." Nevertheless, as with the rest of the animal kingdom, their persons are their most valuable media for display. As only Veblen could put it:

> For this purpose no line of consumption affords a more apt
> illustration than expenditure on dress. It is especially the rule
> of the conspicuous waste of goods that finds expression in
> dress, although the other, related principles of pecuniary re-

pute are also exemplified in the same contrivances. Other
methods of putting one's pecuniary standing in evidence
serve their end effectually, and other methods are in vogue
always and everywhere; but expenditure on dress has this advantage over most other methods, that our apparel is always
in evidence and affords an indication of our pecuniary standing to all observers at the first glance (Veblen 1973:119).

Just as animals display with their coats and their plumage, humans display with their clothing—at Veblen's point in history by
employing a great deal of animal coats and plumage! The major
difference between animals and humans lies in the consciousness
of esteem. Anyone who has observed the bearing of a gorilla, dog,
or a rutting bull elk knows that it appears, at least, as if these animals have self-esteem. They prominently display themselves and
their versions of wealth.

Humans, on the other hand and by their own admission, are
conscious of their need for considerable quantities of esteem. The
importance of esteem to the human psyche is indicated by its residence in Maslow's hierarchy of needs. And in fact, the liquidating class practices the same *behavior* as the animals, issues of consciousness aside. While the neoclassical economists crow about
"economic man," or *Homo economicus* (that calculating, utility-
maximizing profiteer), the display of wealth is one trait that does
little to distinguish *Homo* from the other species.

Why then persecute the liquidating class? They really can't
help it; they are driven by the most basic, animal instincts. A more
sensible perspective would be pity. With all their basic needs
met in abundance, liquidators could be out smelling roses, paint-
ing landscapes, or getting closer to God. In Maslow's terms, they
could be self-actualizing. Instead, they are mired in their liquidat-

ing habits. They can't stop, because if they do, others will get ahead, and they will lose their self-esteem. It is a phenomenon sufficiently pathetic to drive some of its practitioners into physical and psychological ruin, much as the display-crazy robin may pursue its red-breasted reflection to a mortal encounter with the patio door.

Natural selection, which has apparently played a key role in the instinct to display wealth, does not operate exclusively on individuals, however. As Veblen noted, "The evolution of social structure has been a process of natural selection of institutions." How does such a process occur without a societal analogy to DNA? It is easy to see how self-destructive societal traits would be weeded out, but what is the mechanism to make positive societal traits inheritable? Some readers might recall old Jean-Baptiste Pierre de Monet de Lamarck—the Chevalier de Lamarck, or just Lamarck for short! He was the French naturalist who thought that physical traits could be acquired through the exigencies of lifestyle, then somehow passed on to offspring. While this theory was shot down and replaced by theories of genetic inheritance, "it is widely accepted that socioeconomic evolution can be Lamarckian" (Hodgson 1996:40). Common sense. Attitudes and institutions adapt to the times and are passed on to or imitated by succeeding generations, especially if the socioeconomic conditions creating the need for the adaptation remain.

Beyond social institutions, the survival of the fittest applies to species themselves; only species that fit well with their environment survive. Species whose members don't reproduce effectively go extinct, as do species whose members tend to overpopulate and despoil their environments. Perhaps this is where *Homo* will prove its *sapience* after all. If we can understand what motivates us, we should be able to modify the behaviors that threaten us, right? We should be able to adopt the attitudes and institutions necessary to fit with our environment, neither providing too few offspring to perpetuate the species nor liquidating too much of the environment for personal gain, nor toxifying the environment in the process. We should be able to get beyond the level of self-esteem and on to the business of self-actualization whereby we are true to our nature, which presumably includes being a conscientious species.

Now we face one of the ancient questions of philosophy. Are we predestined to behave a certain way, or do we have free will? Even if we know that excessive liquidation is wrong, can we do anything to stop it, given our instinctive desire to display wealth?

For an ecologist, there appears to be no stronger force in life than that of natural selection which, applied to individuals or species, produces profoundly powerful adaptations. And that is where the hope lies for the liquidating class and their grandkids, and for the rest of us and ours, because perhaps we have more than an individual instinct to survive and reproduce. Perhaps as a species with—we are told—anywhere from 130,000 to two million years of evolution (Wong 1998), the development of a conscious and conscientious mind has provided us with the supreme adaptation for the survival of the species. Yes, we are driven to display wealth for the sake of reproduction at the individual level. But our nations are driven to survive on the national level and our cultures are driven to survive on the cultural level, often at the expense of individual wealth. Conscious, planned, and coordinated effort goes into these survival processes. Whether it is evolved, an incidental byproduct of neurological evolution, or a gift from God, we appear to have the ability to organize societies and defeat some of the basic, individual instincts when necessary for the greater good. So who is to say that planning for a steady state economy is a lost cause, and that *Homo economicus* cannot compute beyond his own checking account? Or who is to say that we cannot self-actualize—become true to our conscientious nature—on a societal scale?

We still haven't come far in answering the question of how a democratic society dissuades its members from wastefully liquidating the grandkids' environment. As a first step, we have identified wasteful liquidation for display purposes as an animal instinct that the liquidating class abides by, having satisfied the lower levels of Maslow's hierarchy. As a second step, perhaps it will help to identify an apparent shortcoming of Veblen's otherwise remarkably insightful *Theory of the Leisure Class*. Veblen thought that "With the exception of the instinct of self-preservation, the propensity for emulation [by displaying wealth] is probably the strongest and most alert and persistent of the economic motives proper." Perhaps he dismissed the reproductive instinct as non-"economic," yet one cannot understand the penchant to display wealth without understanding the value of such display to reproductive success. Maslow's hierarchy is more consistent with evolutionary theory; the display of wealth is, first and foremost, a strategy for meeting reproductive needs (including the attendant aspects of love and affection), which precede the need for self-esteem. Animals like elk, peacocks, and humans display their wealth in order to attract partners for the sake of reproduction. We can agree with Veblen that the display of wealth by humans has the value of building esteem, but such value is additional to the primary, reproductive, love-and-affection value.

In most species, including humans, males do most of the displaying and courting, while females do most of the selecting and accepting. This gives the ecologically economic woman a special role to play in the steady state revolution in public opinion, a role that is at once a privilege and a burden. The role is to reject suitors of the liquidating class. It is a privilege because it makes it possible for the woman to steer society, and a burden to the extent that it tests the woman's own self-esteem. But the woman is endowed with other instincts, including a mothering instinct that produces great powers of the will. Darwin's contemporary, Alfred Wallace, believed that mate selection by intelligent women could select for societal qualities. The intelligent woman who understands that the liquidating man—for the sake of animal lust and a greedy level of esteem—jeopardizes the grandchildren's existence with his liquidating behavior, will surely reject such a suitor. With Maslow's third need unmet, the rejected suitor will modify his behavior accordingly.

While a man's superfluous display may be interpreted as an evolved instinct run amuck, a woman's selection of such display may be interpreted likewise. This latter form of running amuck, or "escalation," was noted in birds by the brilliant Darwinian, Ronald Fisher. In this theory, the female's selection of male gaudiness

> could start from a "sensible" choice and then cut loose from its utilitarian moorings to soar off into the realms of extravagance. Imagine, say, that longer-than-normal tails help the males to fly better, so female preference for ever-longer tails is favoured by natural selection; eventually they become a downright encumbrance, but female preference for them is by that time sufficiently widespread to take off under its own sexually-selected steam (Cronin 1991:202).

Lest this argument become chauvinistic, it does not put the onus for a steady state revolution exclusively or even primarily on women. While many animal species are genetically "hard-wired," with virtually no exception to male display and female choice, women are not confined to waiting and watching for men to come along and display. They may themselves do the displaying, seeking the acceptance of a specific mate or a certain type—Darwin himself noted that male choice (of displaying females) was not uncommon in humans. Even women who choose to take the traditional "passive" role do quite a bit of displaying in the process with clothing, jewelry, and various forms of property. So men too are responsible for their actions as the targets of gaudy courtship, and should likewise spurn women of the liquidating class.

As alluded to in chapter 6, people with a lot of money are not necessarily liquidators. For example, a man with a lot of money may live in a small house and ride the bus to work. He saves his money or spends it on charitable works. He prefers not to invest it, because investment provides firms with capital and is therefore one of the forces driving economic bloating. Disingenuous women exist that will gladly fulfill the man's needs for love and affection in order to have access to the man's money, whereupon liquidating behavior will commence. For example, the woman may demand a large house, gas-guzzling car, continual vacationing—liquidation in all its profligate forms. The steady state man will shun these types of women, and again, the same situation may arise with the roles reversed.

Women will generally not marry men whom they pity, and vice versa. When the liquidator has to resort to purchasing limousine service or spending a thousand dollars on a bottle of wine to win amorism or admiration, we are offered a rather pathetic spectacle: the liquidator blindly following his evolutionary programming to a haywired extreme. Yet if the man has no idea what his actions mean to the grandkids, then he shouldn't be viewed with contempt. For despite such ignorance, the man may have redeeming features. At this point the ecologically economic woman will attempt to educate the liquidator and wait for a response (like a date in a regular car and a ten-dollar bottle of wine). If there is none, then revulsion becomes the appropriate behavioral response. Again, the genders may be reversed.

If revulsion seems harsh, it may help to review in some detail the impact of liquidating behavior on the grandkids' prospects. First of all, liquidators tend to have large estates. Large estates use up space, requiring more infrastructure and transportation. Much of the wildlife habitat of an estate is converted to structures or to monocultured landscapes. The buildings use up needless amounts of lumber, quarried rock, minerals, and other natural resources—construction spending represents about 14 percent of gross national product (Stein and Foss 1995). The annual energy consumption of mansions is outlandish. What such properties amount to is the extraction of valuable materials and the destruction of lands from which the materials are obtained, often in far-off places. In other words, the construction and maintenance of such estates results in the liquidation of the grandkids' natural environment. Consider the California residence of William Randolph Hearst, the publishing magnate:

> Hearst's domain began with a fifty-mile strip of oceanfront property midway between Los Angeles and San Francisco,

and stretched into the mountains, encompassing a total of two hundred forty thousand acres. The construction of the gardens alone cost a reported one million dollars. And like the rest of the estate, these were never finished. Squads of full-time landscape architects and gardeners were kept at work, altering and improving the floral displays. While on a trip Hearst was enchanted by the smell of daphne. He wired his chief gardener, Nigel Keep, to plant a row of the aromatic shrub all around the main castle. Keep had to buy up every single available daphne in the state of California at a cost of twelve thousand dollars to fulfill the chief's wish. Once, Keep and his crew worked under floodlights through the night so that Hearst's guests could awaken on Easter morning to see the castle surrounded by thousands of blooming Easter lilies (Thorndike 1976:221–222).

I used the phrase "California residence"—where the swimming pool alone cost more than a million dollars—because Hearst's total estate actually included six other castles around the world. Much of his annual $15 million consumption expenditure went to making these other properties as grandiose as they could also be.

Aside from residence, liquidators tend to drive huge cars that get awful gas mileage. They thus use more metal and leave a lesser stock of petroleum to be tapped, putting the pressure on scientists to find a sustainable energy source, perhaps forcing bad decisions. They pollute disproportionately in the process. Of course, some forms of transportation are more illustrative than others, and there is a rich history of liquidation via transportation. The imagination can be tested by the following description (which here lacks its attendant photographs):

As status symbols, railroad cars were unsurpassed. George M. Pullman, who built most of them, furnished for himself the *Monitor*, whose observation lounge appears on the opposite page. As a special feature, the *Monitor* had its own organ. The *Marchesa* (middle) had a luxurious barber chair under a dome of colored glass. Above is the rear platform of the *Iolanthe*, built for a private rental pool (Thorndike 1976:111).

There is plenty of room to doubt the primacy of railroad cars as status symbols, however. Although the post-matinee dinner arrangement must have been simply preposterous to guests number 29–40, consider the 380-foot "yacht" of Stavros Niarchos:

> The *Atlantis* has a dining room for twenty-eight, a movie theater for forty, a swimming pool, and twelve guest suites. For getting about in all elements, it carries two speedboats and two automobiles, and has a helicopter pad (Thorndike 1976:115).

The attire of liquidators is unsurpassed in quantity and quality. In other words, liquidators require an inordinate production of hard-to-find fibers, leathers, and furs, which means that they leave less land for wildlife and for the grandkids.

> Berry Wall, who set the pace as a boulevardier . . . was said to have had five hundred outfits to choose from. At Saratoga, on a bet, he once made his appearance during a single day in forty changes of costume (Thorndike 1976:19).

Clothing is not the only way to waste plant and animal materials. Consider "Ursa Major," the home of basketball legend Wilt Chamberlain:

Never one for understated elegance, Chamberlain kicked off
a storm of protest when he let it be known that the spread in
the sunken conversation pit in his bedroom was fashioned
from the muzzles of seventeen thousand Arctic wolves. Chamberlain, who bought up an entire year's supply to be used as
design accents in his home, defended himself by saying that
the killing of the wolves was necessary to maintain Alaska's
ecological balance (Thorndike 1976:212).

Liquidators accumulate large, wasteful items, using up storage
space in trivial pursuit. Texas businessman Stanley Marsh half-
buried a row of Cadillacs in a wheat field, rear ends thrust to the
heavens. "He just likes to see how people look and hear what they
saw when they see his 'Cadillac Ranch'" (Thorndike 1976:223).
     Most liquidators combine the modes of liquidation with ease.
Consider Paul Allen, one of the original Microsoft partners:

> He toured Europe, did scuba diving, and picked up the elec-
> tric guitar. He constructed a country estate near Seattle, in-
> cluding two swimming pools and an indoor basketball court,
> with a Maserati and four Ferraris parked in the garage. He
> also bought a private jet and a 150-foot yacht. Allen indulged
> his passion for basketball by acquiring the Portland Trail
> Blazers basketball team (Klepper and Gunther 1996:130).

Freakish extremes are useful for illustrating principles in all
economies. In the economy of nature, for example, the freakish
crocodile can turn on its mates' nests, plundering the nesting
habitat and consuming the eggs. While most male crocodiles in-
stinctively give wide berth to nests, the freakish monster can liquidate entire generations of crocodiles. But there are many be-

haviors that lie between monstrous and benign. Liquidators don't have to consume like a William Randolph Hearst to jeopardize the grandkids' inheritance.

In chapter 6 the liquidating class was defined as the upper one percentile in personal consumption expenditure, with a promise of future explanation for which the time has come. First of all, we have to start somewhere. We could designate the top percentile as 1, 5, 10, or even 95, because "liquidator" is a relative term. As we encompass more and more of the population, however, the implications become more and more austere. And that is not good for a revolution in public opinion. But to turn the tables of public opinion on the upper one percentile should not challenge the fair-play ethics of many. After all, approximately 62 percent of the annual increase in American wealth goes to the one percent of Americans whose per capita net worth is already greater than $2.35 million (Zepezauer and Naiman 1996). They own almost half of the nation's wealth (Hacker 1997), as much as that owned by the bottom 90 percent of the population! These 2.7 million Americans have as much money as the 240 million Americans whose per capita net worth is less than $340,000, and their incomes have more than doubled since 1979 (Frank 1999).

Furthermore, such wealthy folk generally comprise the chief executive officers and board members of large corporations that are subsidized by the rest of us. The aviation industry, for example, is subsidized to the tune of $5.5 billion per year. Mining corporations get $3.5 billion per year, while oil and gas company tax breaks amount to $2.4 billion (Zepezauer and Naiman 1996).

Clearly these figures pertaining to income and net worth are not the same as personal consumption expenditures, but just as clearly, the two are closely aligned. Veblen described the incredible lengths taken by men and women to display wealth via conspicuous consumption, Maslow provided a motivational theory to explain why this is so, and evolutionary theory reveals that such motivation is deeply rooted in the animal kingdom. Conspicuous, wasteful consumption is the result of an animal urge to display, an urge that is presumably felt by all, but to freakish extent by some who eschew self-actualization for insatiable self-esteem. All else equal in terms of social context, those who have the strongest urge are driven to make the most money in order to consume most conspicuously, so income and wealth are certainly related to personal consumption expenditure. That is why wealthy misers are viewed as nonconformists.

Has the correlation of personal consumption expenditures and income been published? Not that I am aware of, having searched for it in academia and having contacted the U.S. Bureau of Economic Analysis as well as the U.S. Bureau of Labor Statistics. The latter does have statistics on both factors, but for some reason doesn't correlate them. Nor can one accurately correlate the factors with their published data, which are only provided in quintiles (groups encompassing 20 percent) or other large categories. Therefore their publications demonstrate only the general relationship between expenditure and income. For example, while 1994 tax filers from the lowest income quintile spent $759 per year on apparel, filers from the highest quintile spent $3,402. For entertainment, the figures were $709 and $3,401, respectively. Filers in the $5,000 to $10,000 income bracket spent $182 on personal care products and services, compared to $769 spent by filers in the over $70,000 income bracket. Unfortunately, these data tell almost nothing about what the upper *one* percentile spends. One can purchase the data set to achieve more statistical precision, but only a compromised version in which incomes over $70,000 are lumped into a single category.

The difficulty encountered in ascertaining the income/expenditure correlation supports the observation of Andrew Hacker in *Money* (1997:28), "People are more defensive about money than any other subject, with the possible exception of the way they raise their children." While liquidators like their egos secretly stroked in public among nameless strangers, or at private gatherings of similarly pompous acquaintances, they do not like their financial lives analyzed with academic rigor, especially when the potential exists to relate financial data to a narcissistic disregard of posterity. About all we can do is find clues here and there, like from tax returns. In a recent year, for example, there were 225 taxpayers with incomes in excess of a million dollars who claimed medical deductions (Hacker 1997). How much did these truly rich folk spend on medical bills? An average of $77,700! Maybe money is hard on your health, contrary to what economists have always taught. Or maybe a lot of these "medical" bills were for nose jobs, face lifts, and massages. Care to guess?

One thing is for sure; you have to be rich to be a liquidator. So by virtual default, there is a correlation of wealth to liquidating behavior. Nevertheless and as previously acknowledged, there *are* people with large amounts of money who do *not* embody the spirit of the liquidating class, including philanthropists and misers. Perhaps that is the beauty of the concept, from the perspective of operationalizing a steady state revolution in public opinion. If we had to know what a person's net worth was, or if we had to analyze the person's annual expenditure report for the sake of classification, it would be rather hopeless. But the liquidating class is readily identifiable because of the very conspicuousness of its consumption. Freakish examples aside, the liquidator is the man with the 10,000-square-foot home, the 100-foot swimming pool, and the expansive landscape with Veblen's "circuitous drive laid across level ground." The liquidator is the woman who, following her $200 weekly massage, dons her mink coat, proceeds in her Cadillac to Antoine's, and orders the caviar. As for the one percent, we don't need to fall into the rigor trap of precision. Just think of driving around in a large city where all levels of wealth are fairly represented. Out of a hundred other motorists, the one with the most expensive car is the liquidator. Out of a hundred homes, the one displaying the most conspicuous consumption belongs to the liquidator. If your estimate is off by a few percentage points, it is close enough; the almost-liquidators do quite a bit of liquidating themselves.

The point is, at this early stage in the steady state revolution in public opinion, there is little need to begrudge a man his 2,000-square-foot home, his 5-foot bird bath, or his square lawn and straight driveway. Nor should we begrudge the woman who gets her $20 chiropractic adjustment, dons the fake fur coat, and heads off in the Oldsmobile for the monthly halibut dinner at Red Lobster. There are bigger fish to fry, and we need the amorphic class to help catch them. Mistakes in identification will be made, of course, but it's not like we'll be burning the misidentified at the stake or sending them to Siberia. Besides, as people get to know other people and the exceptional circumstances surrounding their consumption habits, the liquidators will congeal on the surface.

Although this chapter has focused on those characteristics of the liquidating class that have a negative impact on our grandkids' futures, there are other, more immediate rationales for finding the liquidator's company objectionable and for deeming the liquidator's residence a poor option for child-rearing. For one thing, the liquidating class seems to be characterized by a certain psychopathology, a liquidation syndrome as it were. We have already noted the freakish and monstrous traits of conspicuous consumption, but those were concerned with physical display and natural capital liquidation. Here we are concerned with the insidious psychological phenomena related to those traits.

Liquidation syndrome is readily indicated by conspicuous consumption, and its pathology entails a sort of motivational retardation. Liquidators seem obsessed with the third and fourth levels of Maslow's hierarchy, scarcely removed from the rest of the animal kingdom. Liquidators eschew the fifth or self-actualization level, which is where the psychologically healthy reside, according to Maslow. In the fifth level, one moves beyond conspicuous consumption to "become everything that one is capable of becoming" (Maslow 1954:92).

How does one "be all that one can be?" Some master spelunking, some sculpt, some join the Army Reserves; everyone has unique interests and abilities. Nevertheless, several common features of self-actualizing people have been identified, and it is striking how these features juxtapose those of the liquidating class. For example, Maslow (1954:208) found that, "Their behavior is marked by simplicity and naturalness, and by lack of artificiality or straining for effect." In this one sentence lie the opposites of liquidation and conspicuous consumption. And, for the self-actualizing:

> There are some differences in choice of beautiful objects. Some subjects go primarily to nature. For others it is primarily children, and for a few subjects it has been primarily great

music; but it may certainly be said that they derive ecstasy, inspiration, and strength from the basic experiences of life. No one of them, for instance, will get this same sort of reaction from going to a night club or getting a lot of money or having a good time at a party (Maslow 1954:215).

Self-actualizers, according to Maslow, are universally creative, so that the lack of creativity is a sure sign that self-actualization has not been engaged. Conspicuous consumption hardly constitutes creativity— half-buried Cadillacs notwithstanding.

Closely related to creativity is the penchant for self-actualizing people to be inquisitive. This trait combined with one other—a concern for the welfare of humankind present and future—leads the self-actualizing person to acquire knowledge to use in betterment of the human prospect. Consumption, on the other hand, amounts to buying the products of someone else's knowledge, and conspicuous consumption is a threat to the grandkids.

Although the liquidator's pathology clearly entails a "groveling" in Maslow's fourth level relative to self-actualizing in the fifth, we can only guess about the underlying causes. For some liquidators, the answer may lie in Maslow's (1954:98) observation that "There are some people in whom, for instance, self-esteem seems to be more important than love." He called this the most common reversal in the hierarchy of needs and thought it was usually due to a lack of confidence. This brings us back to the limousine service and the thousand-dollar bottle of wine: instead of a loving relationship building the suitor's self-esteem, it is the suitor's self-esteem building love. But for the young lady or man in search of a life partner, what kind of love would this be? Love so embellished might even border on revenge. Andrew Hacker

(1997:206) interviewed some of the wealthiest people and biggest spenders in America to get some insight on the factors motivating them. One answered:

> Each year I am listed in a national magazine as one of the wealthiest people in this country. . . . Frankly, it means a lot to me to be up there. It's like winning an Academy Award or Nobel Prize or the Medal of Honor. And something else. When I was young, I was regarded as a nerd, especially by the girls, who wouldn't give me the time of day. They all know who I am now and what I've attained. There was one in particular . . . [Thankfully, Hacker's quote stops there].

Maslow's work also suggests that liquidators are afraid of the uncontrollable, natural world and therefore surround themselves with a superfluity of man-made objects. In other words, liquidators are manipulators and controllers, all the more reason to stay out of a relationship with one.

Of course, one may wonder how we can be so sure that the liquidator is not already operating at the fifth level. Perhaps for some liquidators, there *is* little meaning in life beyond consumption, so that being *all* that one can be amounts to *conspicuous* consumption. Yet with all the art, literature, music, religion, science, and adventure that other folks have embraced—often on modest budgets—treating consumption as the coup de grâce of one's being strongly suggests mental deficiency.

We have seen what the liquidating class means to the grandkids' prospects, and have noted that liquidators tend to have serious intellectual and social shortcomings from the start—reason enough to shun the liquidating suitor. However, even for liquidators who don't come with a prepackaged pathology, the liquidating lifestyle may produce one. Luxury, especially, has long been known to spoil and weaken its practitioners. The Lebanese poet Kahlil Gibran wrote about the "lust for comfort, that stealthy thing that enters the house a guest, and then becomes a host, and then a master." According to Veblen, liquidators also tend to acquire a dullness of wit that accompanies complacency, with stagnating societal effects:

> The leisure class is in great measure sheltered from the stress of those economic exigencies which prevail in any modern, highly organized industrial community. The exigencies of the struggle for the means of life are less exacting for this class than for any other; and as a consequence of this privileged position we should expect to find it one of the least responsive of the classes of society to the demands which the situation makes for a further growth of institutions. . . . The office of the leisure class in social evolution is to retard the movement and to conserve what is obsolescent (Veblen 1973:137).

Veblen's observation wasn't just a function of the Gilded Age. As Martin Marty (1999:188) observed, "Regularly, critics observe that as North Americans get more and consume more, they are increasingly unsatisfied spiritually and thus paralyzed when it comes to making difficult decisions and taking daring steps."

To summarize, liquidators exhibit a syndrome that separates them from healthy, self-actualizing people of similar wealth. Whatever the pathology, all liquidators are either ignorant of or ignore the consequences of their behavior for the grandkids. The perspective most appropriate for the ignorant liquidator is pity, while the perspective most appropriate for the knowing yet greedy liquidator is revulsion. The ignorant may be educated to the point of self-actualization, while the greedy may only be reviled, not violently or threateningly, but clearly.

This discussion has focused on the mating relationship between males and females because it has such powerful potential for perspective building, but pity or revulsion should be applied to the liquidating class in all types of social situations. Otherwise, the considerable percentage of old, homosexual, or already-married liquidators shall have no social incentive to modify their liquidating behavior.

# RELATIONS WITH THE
# STEADY STATE CLASS

8

To effect the steady state revolution in public opinion, the primary shift in the majority's perception involves the liquidating class, which is the problematic class in terms of economic bloating. However, it may also help to develop a particular perspective of the steady state class, a perspective that rewards the membership thereof. Such a perspective will encourage steady staters to remain steady staters, and will encourage amorphs to temper their consumption.

In chapter 6, the steady state class was defined as the bottom 80 percent in terms of personal consumption expenditures. This category roughly corresponds to the categories of "poor" and "middle class" in monetary terms. Why not use a steady state criterion that includes only the bottom 70 percent, 50 percent, or only the poor? First of all, not everyone in the amorphic class will participate in the steady state revolution in public opinion, so it will help to have a large majority classified as steady staters from the start. However, that doesn't make the 80 percent criterion a cheap political trick. Approximately 99 percent of the annual increase in Americans' wealth goes to the 20 percent of the population that is already the most wealthy! Furthermore, the discrepancy in wealth distribution is a worsening trend. While the average income of the 80 percent of Americans who are nonmanagerial has declined over the past twenty years, the average income of the remaining twenty percent has risen (Zepezauer and Naiman 1996).

The relationship between wealth and consumption was discussed in chapter 7. It is not absolute, but it clearly exists. And just as there are political and economic rationales for the bottom 80 percent in income to unite against "wealthfare"—the subsidization of the rich—there are social rationales for the bottom 80 percent in consumption to unite against the conspicuous consumption of the liquidating class. After all, we have the majority of grandkids whose prospects are darkened by the liquidation of the natural environment.

In developing a perspective of the steady state class, it may help to review some of the prospects produced by their consumptive behavior. There are no freakish examples to report here; steady staters simply have small houses and lots, taking up less space and leaving more for others. Their small houses and lots require less infrastructure and less commuting. Because they drive small cars that get good gas mileage, they leave a greater stock of petroleum to be tapped while scientists grope for a sustainable energy source. They also pollute less. Many of them ride bikes or use public transit. Because they don't have a different wardrobe for every occasion, they require less production of fiber, leather, and fur, which means that they leave more land for wildlife and for the grandkids. They don't accumulate large, wasteful items, thus saving storage space and tempering the traffic in trivial pursuits like half-burying Cadillacs. Basically, every form of conspicuous consumption practiced by the liquidating class is either avoided or practiced to a far less conspicuous degree by the steady state class. In other words, while the liquidator jeopardizes the grandkids' inheritance, the steady stater preserves it. For all the above, do we not owe the steady staters some reverence, or at least some gratitude?

Just as the issue of pity versus revulsion could only be resolved by determining the liquidators' awareness of their impacts, so it is with the issue of gratitude versus reverence for steady staters. The wide range of monetary wealth possessed by steady staters means that there is a wide range of consumption possibilities. If the veritably poor steady stater, upon receiving her part-time minimum wage paycheck, blows it on a pair of inexpensive earrings, she is probably not a steady stater at heart. If given the chance, she would, perhaps, blow a full-time maximum wage paycheck on a pair of splendiferous earrings. However, there is always the chance that her need for self-esteem is met by the modest earrings, and that she would still purchase the same inexpensive pair at the higher wage. Just as we do not automatically revolt in disgust from liquidators until we know if they know better, why not give the poor woman the benefit of the doubt? After all, she is a steady stater in effect, if not in intention, and that is the main thing as far as the grandkids are concerned. Almost everyone in society, including undisciplined yet understanding amorphs and liquidators, should find it easy to show her gratitude. After all, even the liquidating class has its grandkids (who should be neither pitied nor repulsed prior to exhibiting their own consumption habits). Only pitiful ignorami among the liquidating class will feel revulsion for the poor woman based on her cheap earrings or lack of earrings.

Perhaps the steady state spirit of the poor can be gauged to some extent by number of offspring. Because economic bloating is a function of population size and per capita consumption, poor people with plentiful children are not convincingly steady statish. Again, however, if the poor couple with many children has not been educated about the problem of economic bloating, they should not be viewed with the slightest revulsion, but with a combination of pity and gratitude. Pity for the excessive financial burden, and gratitude because even a hundred poor children will consume less than will a tenth of one liquidator. The poor couple with two or less children, on the other hand, show a real understanding of the concept of carrying capacity (even if only at the family scale) and therefore evince a steady state spirit; they should be cherished.

While education is a good criterion for assessing the turpitude of consumptive behavior, it cannot be equally applied to liquidators and the poor subset of steady staters. The liquidating class is wealthy, and the wealthy are far more educated than the poor. They often attend private schools, are assisted by private tutors, and usually attend college. Family associates typically include a few intellectual elite, and liquidator estates often contain massive libraries replete with classic literature, presumably including many references to the classical economists like Malthus and Mill, if not the works of such classicists themselves. At the very least, the liquidator's secure environment is fertile grounds for the seed of common sense, a seed that requires little nourishment to produce the awareness that resource liquidation jeopardizes the grandkids' future.

The poor subset of the steady state class, on the other hand, is characterized by few books, shoddy schools, and scant intellectual contact. Expecting the members of this subset to be versed in economics, much less ecological economics, would be like expecting street smarts from the liquidator. The application of this distinction is not to presume a steady state awareness by the poor based upon less evidence than that required of the wealthy. Instead, when steady state awareness *is* apparent, the level of reverence granted the steady stater should increase with the steady stater's poverty. As difficult as it might be for a liquidator to curb his consumption, that challenge pales in comparison to the poor man's conscious approval of his own meager consumption.

This points out a fundamental distinction between the poor subset of the steady state class and all others in society. While there is no way for the poor to leave the steady state class, the most moneyed of the steady staters may join the amorphic class by devoting a higher proportion of their money to conspicuous consumption. Any amorph may join the steady state class by tempering consumption, while the most moneyed amorphs may join the liquidating class via increasingly conspicuous consumption. As a whole, the liquidating class has the most options. Each and every member may join the amorphic class by tempering consumption to a moderate degree, or even the steady state class by tempering consumption to a major degree.

Of course, this money-based distinction is strictly valid only in the short term. In the United States, the poor man may work his way up monetarily, whereupon his true consumptive colors will shine. Take Merle Haggard, one of my longtime favorite singers. Merle was born in a railroad car, and when he sings a song about struggling in poverty—as he often does—you can feel the revenuer comin' round the mountain. But he is one of those rarities in American pop culture that converted his talent into riches, and with disillusioning results. Merle likes the countryside, so he stayed off Nob Hill. Instead, he bought a $700,000 mansion on 180 acres! His $100,000 traveling bus sits in the garage, and his $50,000 model train collection sits in the playroom (all in 1976 dollars). Of course, he didn't have the advantage of a high-class education, so revulsion would be inappropriate. And, given the long lean years he put in, we should never begrudge him a little comfort. But $50,000 on toy trains! For the sake of the grandkids, let's hope Merle lays off the "Rainbow Stew" he used to sing about.

The promising combination of thrifty parents and a solid education is no insurance against conspicuous consumption, either, as the singer Elton John exemplifies:

> The son of an RAF squadron leader who was so strict he
> would not allow his son to purchase a mohair sweater favored
> by the young English toffs of the 1960's, John's passion now
> is buying things. Exotic eye glasses are one of his trademarks,
> and John does not stint. He has forty-thousand-dollars' worth.
> He owns pairs ringed with mink, encrusted with diamonds,
> and equipped with their own windshield wipers. One pair is
> fitted with miniature light bulbs, which spell out "ELTON"
> when turned on. His shopping sprees are legendary. He gave
> his manager an eighty-thousand-dollar yacht, and then threw
> in a ten-thousand-dollar Fabergé clock. His agent received a
> Rolls-Royce (Thorndike 1976:208–209).

At least Elton John gives things away, but giving away such extravagant objects probably serves to spread the behavior of conspicuous consumption; indeed, such a tendency was parcel to

Veblen's theory. (To be fair, John has been quite charitable to the poor as well as to the rich.)

But back to the role of social relations in the steady state revolution in public opinion. According to our evolutionary model, as enhanced by Veblen and Maslow, females are attracted to the display of wealth primarily because the display is a sign of strength. This is consistent with sociologists' findings that women care less about the aesthetic features of a man's face or body than about the strength the man's presence exudes, in whatever form. This is where the ecologically economic, liberated, and thinking woman has the opportunity to let her brain overcome her animal instincts. Splendiferous accouterment and pretentious residence must not be mistaken for strength, but rather for the weakness that they breed and perhaps even for the psychological deficiencies associated with liquidator syndrome. Meanwhile, the inherent strength of the steady stater should be acknowledged. What, if not strength, allows one to survive in the world's most capitalistic society with little money? Perhaps related traits like physical endurance and mental toughness. Given that life is a continual series of microeconomic decisions, "luck" is seldom a factor. Nor do the poor man and rich man start out on the same playing field, testing strength like linemen in a football game. Usually the wealthy man started with a silver spoon, or at least with enough money to multiply his money, which is properly to be expected, not viewed as a sign of strength. The ecologically economic woman avoids the intellectual mistake of ascribing less wealth to less strength.

Why should an increase in wealth, say from a small fortune to opulent riches, not be viewed as a sign of strength? The answer derives from the old maxim, "It takes money to make money."

Exceptional cases certainly exist (like Merle Haggard emerging from the boxcar of his youth), but this sage observation has stood the test of time because of its economic validity. Classical, neo-classical, and Marxist economists have all agreed on the matter; capitalism systematically makes the rich richer and the poor poorer. What follows is a corollary: In a bloating economy, anyone starting out with money and failing to accumulate more money must be a hapless half-wit. The ecologically economic woman is not fooled into thinking that a man's growing wealth is a sign of exceptional intelligence. It would rather be a sign of exceptional idiocy if the moneyed man's wealth was declining. Unless of course the fellow was self-actualizing by consciously choosing a reduction in wealth—a true sign of strength to the ecologically economic woman.

The obverse of the takes-money maxim is, "It takes a lack of money not to make money." The poor man shows nothing by his poverty except a tendency to adhere to the economic odds. Obviously, the knowledge of this cannot convert abject poverty into an attractive feature. But the ecologically economic woman also knows that, in the United States, there is little to prevent the poor man from attaining a *secure* financial stature. The threshold into *riches* is relatively inaccessible, but within the lower to middle classes, people move up and down the scale of wealth when motivated to do so, for example by the affection (Maslow's third level) of a steady state woman or by the esteem (Maslow's fourth level) afforded to membership in the steady state class during a steady state revolution. Indeed, this is one of the defining characteristics of the American socioeconomic scene. It is also what separates a democracy from an aristocracy.

This phenomenon is particularly applicable to the situation of

the young lady of blue collar class. Traditionally, a significant proportion of such young ladies have been pressured by parents into
seeking a wealthy, or at least a white-collared, suitor. The young
lady may be in love with a strong young man from the "down
in the boondocks," but her association with said young man is
continually hindered by her parents. Eventually and unhappily,
she consorts with a moneyed weakling, and the broken-hearted
suitor takes an antisocial turn.

Whether or not this situation is as common in reality as in the
pulp fiction it permeates, it certainly is not rare. Feminist scholars like Lenore Weitzman have noted that women of the working class continue to face antiquated sex-role pressures, including
the pressure to marry into a higher class. The steady state revolution in public opinion would virtually eliminate this form of
tragedy.

Furthermore, the rapidly changing role of women in the
American workforce alleviates a woman's dependence on male
financial performance. Although signs of gender discrimination
persist in the workforce—most notably in the form of lower
wages for women—the general opening of the workforce to either gender makes it easier for a poor woman to go it alone or to
team with a poor man and help to create a comfortable, steady
state household.

Thus far, this chapter has focused on the poor subset of the
steady state class, at times in stark contrast to the liquidating class.
We have seen much of merit in the poor, at least in effect, and
have perhaps removed some of the social tarnish accumulated
thereon. While the poor have a guaranteed place for our gratitude, the more moneyed of the steady state class deserve their own
special consideration, for the more money such steady staters

have, the more temptation they face to slip into conspicuously consumptive behavior. The fact that they don't warrants special notice. While we may never know how many of the poor are intentional steady staters, we may reasonably assume that some proportion of the more moneyed steady staters are so intentionally.

Evidence may be found, for example, where the successful attorney shuns Nob Hill for a modest lowland flat. This is not proof, only evidence, because she may have chosen to live there in order to devote more income to liquidating investments. But other signs usually accompany the residence. If in the attorney's driveway sits a four-cylinder car with stock parts, and on the curb sits a recycling basket, and on the roof sits a solar panel, surely the lady is a steady stater (and a pretty cool attorney). She should be revered for her strength in the face of peer pressure, her mastery over luxurious temptation, and for the example she sets to other moneyed folk. Conscientious and independent, with no need for the material trappings of "high society," the wealthy steady stater is a prime example of self-actualization.

Just as the nineteenth-century farmer was once the redeemer of American society, so are the steady staters today. The steady state class includes most of the teachers, social workers, janitors, bus drivers, librarians, nurses, plumbers, electricians, carpenters, bricklayers, road workers, linemen, truck drivers, cowboys, police officers, artists, family farmers, and a variety of bureaucrats. It also includes the miners, loggers, ranchers, and others who extract resources for a wage or as a way of life, having nothing to do with the liquidators' demands for *excessive* extraction. In fact, no one typically residing in the middle class has been left out of this list intentionally. The steady state class also includes many attorneys, professors, dentists and doctors, and even some bankers and corporate figureheads who reject the liquidating lifestyle. In other words, the steady state class includes all of the poor, most of the middle class, and a few of the rich. Steady staters comprise the responsibly productive and cooperative sector of the United States, politically and economically. Where liquidation breeds weakness, irresponsibility, and societal obsolescence, steady statism breeds strength, responsibility, and social progress.

Obviously, not everyone in the steady state class fits this description. Some are liquidators at heart and, not having the means to liquidate, seek to escape their dissatisfaction through drugs and alcohol, while others resort to crime. (Oddly enough, so do many of the liquidating class, seemingly for less legitimate reasons.) But aside from such flagrant cases of weakness, the steady stater is a natural subject for gratitude and, in exceptional cases, even for reverence.

# RELATIONS WITH THE AMORPHIC CLASS

Although the personal consumption expenditures used to define the liquidating and steady state classes were not pulled out of a hat, neither were they divined from Providence. Obviously the consumptive behavior of the 79th percentile varies little from that of the 80th percentile, as does the 98th from the 99th. There is, however, a *tremendous* difference between the consumptive behavior of the 79th and the 99th percentile, probably far more than that between the 59th and 79th, or even between the 39th and 79th—certainly enough difference to readily distinguish the liquidating class from the steady state class. Therein lies the value of conceiving an amorphic class and, for that matter, any class.

The value of class designation is further illuminated by considering the alternative, that is, a relational system of classification. One could, for example, propose that each person should perceive as liquidators all others of higher personal consumption expenditure. In a relative sense, each such other would indeed be a liquidator. But this approach opens the door to a number of problematic outcomes. The next-door neighbor, for example, whose consumption is precisely the same as the observer's, would be driven into the observer's liquidator category by the sudden purchase of a higher-grade garden hose. The widow on a pension would be designated a liquidator by several million poverty-stricken Americans lacking even a pension. The Rolls-driving cigar smoker would smugly perceive the yacht-racing Boardwalker as the problem. Clearly, there would be no solidarity afforded by such a system, in which the identification of liquidators would amount to a perpetual slippery slope.

The amorphic class, so named because of a lack of definite shape (morphology), cannot be rigorously identified with luminescent mailboxes or state-provided garments. Even if we had a precise accounting of personal consumption expenditures, we would not know how many dollars were spent on spas versus solar panels. Therein lies another advantage to the concept of the amorphic class. If it is not obvious whether that structure in the back yard is a sauna or a toolshed, leave it be. Chances are, if the owner was a real liquidator, his consumption would be conspicuous enough as to leave no doubt.

This leads back to the comment in chapter 7 on frying bigger fish. The same disunity created by a sliding scale of liquidator identification would result, albeit to a lesser extent, from castigating this amorphic class. And because the majority will be performing the castigation, which will be alarming to the recipients thereof, focusing too low in the personal consumption levels might provoke counter castigation. That is fine to a point. If the upper one percentile wants to castigate the steady state class, who cares? It's not like we've been attending their galas anyway. But castigating the amorphic class is something to be avoided. After all, this class includes many of our doctors and lawyers and such. Although ethically such folks are sworn to perform their services to all in need, common sense says the subconscious has an influence on such performance. Besides, these are folks whose social interaction is generally to be sought. These folks do tend to be highly intelligent, well educated, and generally positive citizens.

Of course, it might not hurt to cast an inquiring *glance* at the structure in back. If it does turn out to be a sauna, the steady stater might proffer, "Wow! That thing must use a lot of energy, eh? That reminds me—I heard the energy company has to increase their coal purchases this year. My aunt lives in West Virginia and she says the coal companies are starting to do what they call 'ridgetop mining.' That's where they basically remove the top portions of the mountains and leave them flat." If the neighbor replies, "Really? I didn't know that. I should probably shut this thing down during the fifty-one weeks of the year that it goes unused," he is probably at least somewhat of a steady stater at heart, and you can look forward to further steady state philosophizing and information exchange. If he replies, "Who the hell cares? It's just a tax write-off anyway," he is clearly a liquidator, if not quite in technical (one percentile) terms, then at heart.

At this point, many a steady stater would suppress a more vulgar version of, "I'm sorry to hear you feel that way. My aunt says those mines are getting out of hand and polluting the rivers, and unless they figure out a sustainable energy source, my grandkids might be depending on that coal. I'd hate to think that peoples' *tax write-offs* are jeopardizing my *grandkids' future!*" Even in this nonvulgar form, the response, in combination with a well-deserved future lack of courtesy, may contribute to a gradual modification of the neighbor's consumptive behavior, especially if the neighbor encounters an increasing number of steady staters in his social pursuits.

Except for such clear-cut opportunities, however, it behooves the steady stater to leave the amorphs alone. Not only do they include doctors and lawyers, but they include many corporate executives, highly successful businessmen, and perhaps worst of all, politicians who depend on the executives and businessmen for campaign support. The fact that the steady state revolution in public opinion does not comprise a coordinated political effort does not preclude a coordinated political *retort* from amorphic wannabe liquidators, who would pose a serious threat to the steady state revolution. Such an effort would muster all the Julian Simons from the academic world to preach their neoclassical canons in public, confusing steady staters of limited economic knowledge. Trickle-down arguments would win the day, as they did during the 1980s when many an ecologically economic policy went by the way.

The amorphic class will also be susceptible to pressure from the liquidating class—the two classes having many social interactions —to squelch the preposterous steady statism. While many in the amorphic class probably view the conspicuous consumption of the liquidating class as preposterous in its own right, their treatment by the steady state class will influence their reaction to the liquidators. The amorph who has had his toolshed mistaken for a sauna (especially by a rogue, vandalous steady stater) is likely to sympathize with the liquidator. On the other hand, the amorph who has been treated with respect by steady staters will pay the lobbying liquidator fleeting attention, especially if he understands the benefits of a steady state economy to the grandkids.

Ironically, clever amorphic wannabe liquidators may be encouraged by the castigation of true liquidators. As the social pressures brought to bear against the liquidating class begin to reduce the consumption thereof, these disingenuous amorphs will be enabled to edge into the liquidating class with scant effort. In the process they win, in an antiquated sense, the esteem they have sought. Yet as they congeal there in Maslow's fourth level, they in turn are subject to the same castigation faced by the liquidators they have replaced. This prospect reveals the potential of the steady state revolution in public opinion to precipitate a positive feedback, whereby consumers are cycled in and out of the liquidating class, first congealing at the top and then melting under the heat of public opinion. This subtle phenomenon is key to stopping the runaway train, and should be carefully cogitated by all readers who may find themselves wondering why we should "only" castigate the upper one percentile.

While Marx announced, "The expropriators are expropriated," Marxism will be irrelevant as the liquidators are liquidated in the midst of a capitalist, steady state democracy. The analogy's weakness is that, while the congealed fat at the top melts under the heat of public opinion, what actually happens is a cooling off of the kettle, i.e., a cooling off of consumption or, voilà, a cooling of the economy. If it cools enough, a steady state economy will result. If it cools fast enough, our grandkids' future is suddenly bright. Wall Street, of course, will be shrieking, "Recession!" But at this point, Americans will awaken from the surreal dream of perpetual economic bloating, take a deep breath, and behold the prospect of a slim, sleek body. Suddenly, and especially if population has stabilized, the pressure will be off! The standard of living will equilibrate, and castigation will cease because the bloating will have stopped.

# EXEMPLARY STEADY STATISM

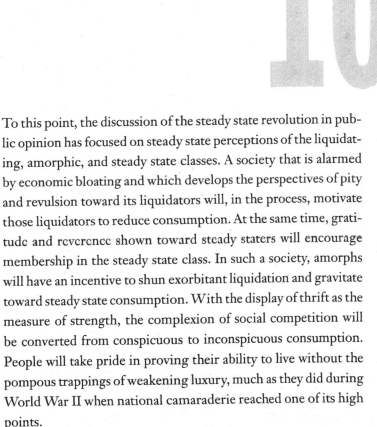

To this point, the discussion of the steady state revolution in public opinion has focused on steady state perceptions of the liquidating, amorphic, and steady state classes. A society that is alarmed by economic bloating and which develops the perspectives of pity and revulsion toward its liquidators will, in the process, motivate those liquidators to reduce consumption. At the same time, gratitude and reverence shown toward steady staters will encourage membership in the steady state class. In such a society, amorphs will have an incentive to shun exorbitant liquidation and gravitate toward steady state consumption. With the display of thrift as the measure of strength, the complexion of social competition will be converted from conspicuous to inconspicuous consumption. People will take pride in proving their ability to live without the pompous trappings of weakening luxury, much as they did during World War II when national camaraderie reached one of its high points.

Furthermore, people will be happier. Their incessant drive to work longer and harder in order to consume ever more—the work and spend cycle documented by Juliet Schor in *The Overworked American*—will subside. Because people will *want* less material cluttering up their lives, less of them will work and those working will work fewer hours. Once again there will be time for soul-building leisure. Not just crammed-in, do-it-all-in-a-week vacations, but everyday simple pleasures with spouses, kids, grandkids, and friends. Time for the self, too. More and more people will self-actualize, taking on their unique, human, conscientious nature. No more shopping and dropping like mall-robots on treadmills.

And of course a lot of money will be saved in the process, which is where the steady state revolution gets tricky. For what is the wealthy, ex-liquidator to do with the money that now piles up at his feet? After all, if he foregoes the conspicuous yacht by inconspicuously giving the money to twenty less-endowed nieces and nephews, each might go out and buy a car, the twenty of which will entail the fabrication of the precise amount of metal contained in the foregone yacht. If he inconspicuously invests it in bonds, the bonds might be used to finance the infrastructure for a liquidating subdivision. Furthermore, if he foregoes his $200 massages, the masseuse may be forced to compete with the dishwasher for a job, thus driving down the wages of the already poor. These are the types of questions that necessitate a consideration of appropriate steady state consumption.

Pope John Paul II knew how important it was for society to make the right consumption decisions. In his 1991 *Centesimus annus*, he laid it on the line:

A given culture reveals its understanding of life through the
choices it makes in production and consumption . . . a great
deal of educational and cultural work is urgently needed, including the education of consumers in the responsible use
of their power of choice. . . . Even the decision to invest in
one place rather than another, in one productive sector rather
than another, is always a moral and cultural choice (from
Marty 1999:189).

At first glance, it seems obvious that all purchases are not equal
in terms of liquidation. Consider the purchase of an enormous
diamond. Diamonds are obtained via the thoroughly liquidating
process of mining. Little diamonds are found routinely, and therefore the purchase of a little diamond requires a relatively small
amount of liquidation. Enormous diamonds are few and far between; to find them entails the liquidation of vast acreages (usually in South Africa). So the purchase of an enormous diamond
is to be repulsed.

Perhaps the liquidator prefers art, and commissions a Salvador
Dalí–type to produce a $100,000 replica of a twisted piece of glass.
That does not seem so bad, because the twisted glass replica requires the consumption of only very small amounts of silica and
boric oxide. As conscientious steady staters, we might not object
to the extent that we would to the diamond purchase. We might
be disappointed, however, if the Salvador Dalí opts, after a few
more such hauls, to purchase the enormous diamond himself,
thus liquidating the same vast South African acreage. Even if the
Dalí is himself a steady stater who gives the money to cousins, the
latter may then go out and buy cars.

This is probably all the permutation required to illustrate that, although some purchases are less directly liquidating, all lead to liquidation. This follows readily from the fact we noted in chapter 3: someone has to produce before anyone can consume. While production is doled out in trophic levels from producers to consumers to fat cats, consumption trickles down from extravagant luxuries to niceties to essentials. When it comes to preserving the grandkids' natural inheritance, nothing is free, not even spending! That is why the liquidating class is identified via personal consumption expenditure to begin with. A penny spent is a penny burned, somewhere in the trickle-down process.

This little cliché is actually quite telling. If a penny spent is a penny burned (in coal, gas, or whatever), and the burning is problematic, then clearly the penny is better saved. Saving—*pure* saving, like hoarding in the cellar—cools down a bloating economy by taking the money out of circulation, where it cannot be employed for consuming and producing purposes. John Maynard Keynes pointed this out with much ado. To the feasibility of such saving we shall soon arrive.

First however, and despite the just-developed argument that all expenditure tends to liquidation, the notion that type of expenditure plays a role in steady statism cannot so easily be dismissed. Consider once more the liquidator who purchased the twisted glass replica from our Salvador Dalí, who, after several such hauls, purchased the enormous diamond. In this case, the original purchase had insignificant liquidating properties, while the secondary purchase had large and direct liquidating properties. If the liquidator had instead purchased the enormous diamond himself, someone besides Salvador Dalí was paid, and that someone may herself have purchased two rubies. In this case, the original purchase *and* the secondary purchase were largely and directly liquidating.

And so we have two seemingly logical arguments that appear paradoxical when juxtaposed. Paradox is not the same as mutual exclusivity, however. The most parsimonious interpretation is that all spending eventually liquidates directly, yet some liquidates more in the process, and therefore some spending is indeed less problematic than others. In other words, the liquidator should not feel "off the hook" for spending the money on the replica instead of the diamond, but the hook may perhaps penetrate a lesser recess of the conscience.

It follows that a brief discussion of consumptive criteria is in order. We have presumably established that price itself is an important and clearly the most objective criterion. All else equal, those who spend more burn more—the more costly an item, the greater its liquidating impact. So to opt for the thousand dollar coat when the hundred dollar coat is identical in all ways except brand name is a liquidating action.

Another criterion is energy expenditure—this would probably be Georgescu-Roegen's criterion of choice. Most energy is yet obtained from fossil fuels. The mining and drilling entailed by fossil fuel extraction is a highly liquidating activity. Some goods are obviously energy intensive, either in their manufacture or in their use. Again the enormous diamond is an example of a good for which a great deal of energy is consumed in the extractive process. Of course, not much energy expenditure is required to show off the diamond.

Other goods require somewhat less energy for their production, but require exorbitant energy consumption in their employment. The clearest example is the recreational or entertainment vehicle. Some liquidators go so far as to purchase race cars and finance the endeavors of the associated drivers and crews. As alluded to in chapter 6, can there be a more recklessly consumptive activity than car racing? The whole enterprise—from the shop to the practice track to the main event—is a perpetual pumping of petroleum. Racing tires, which are practically valueless off the racetrack, are purchased by the dozen, often discarded after a single race, and incinerated into clouds of thick and noxious black smoke. Oil, grease, filters, belts, hoses, bumpers, glass, paint, chrome, vinyl—racing is a smorgasbord of noxious industrial production and consumption. And what type of consumption example does it set for the young and excitable?

Another criterion with which to judge the propriety of consumption is waste. This is a far more subjective criterion, as the steady stater's waste is often the liquidator's esteem. Even among steady staters, waste can be difficult to identify. However, the important thing is not to develop some newfangled wastometer, but to develop the habit of thinking about waste, so that an obvious waste is unable to hide in the fog of relativity. We may be confident, for example, that the vast majority of Americans, employing minimal amounts of reflection, would find a wheatfield of half-buried Cadillacs a wanton waste of land, labor, *and* capital. Such an affront to utility, in the steady state revolution in public opinion, does not even retain the value of sardonic humor which is sometimes derived from another's futility. In the steady state revolution in public opinion, just as conspicuous consumption is replaced with competitively inconspicuous consumption, the lack of concern over wanton waste is converted to a conscious concern for utility.

A closely related criterion is luxury. Luxury has several meanings, including "something inessential but conducive to pleasure and comfort." But very few goods and services are absolutely essential, and there is nothing grossly liquidating about seeking a little pleasure and comfort. Luxury also means "something expensive or hard to obtain." As we have seen, the more expensive an object is, the more liquidating is its purchase. A third definition is "sumptuous living or surroundings," where the adjective "sumptuous" means "of a size or splendor suggesting great expense." This form of luxury, then, connotes excessive liquidation. Synonyms of luxury include "extravagance" and "frill." Luxury, then, combines high expense with waste. Advertisements that boast of luxury should therefore be viewed as supportive of the liquidating lifestyle. In the steady state revolution in public opinion, advertisements of luxury will be viewed with disdain. Luxury will be utterly ugly, and how.

These criteria—expense, energy expenditure, waste, and luxury—may guide steady staters in their purchasing activities. The resulting demand for less expensive, no-frills goods and services will cause producers to adjust their production activities such that resources are conserved. In other words, less will be consumed in the personal consumption process, and less will be consumed in the production process itself. Corporate profits will fall, at which point the corporate world and its economists will protest. They will employ trickle-down economics to threaten wage reductions. In this they will be telling the truth, but not the whole truth if they neglect to add that prices of nonluxurious goods and services will decline as well, due to the lower cost of labor. The purchasing power of a dollar may actually increase for steady staters, who were purchasing the nonluxurious goods to begin with. All things considered, the net economic welfare of the steady state class will be little changed.

Technically, the economic welfare of the liquidating class will decline in such an economy to the extent that the liquidating class originally thrived on corporate profits. However, this should be of little concern to society as a whole. Who cares if a liquidator has to pay more for a luxury item because luxury supplies decline, or if the liquidator has less corporate profit with which to purchase such an item? That will only add economic incentive to the social incentive for tempering liquidation.

At this stage we arrive again at the issue of saving money. Even if the liquidator has less corporate profit with which to consume, she will still have far more than the steady stater, and far more than it would behoove her to spend intemperately, given the social stigma applied to such spending. The liquidator will instead have incentive to save her excess income. But saving—*pure, non-invested saving*—may be hard for the liquidator to swallow because the value of the savings will depreciate with inflation. Inflation is a major deterrent to saving.

Actually, a steady state economy should have an equilibrating effect on prices and money supplies but many factors in addition to GNP movement influence inflation. Ecological economists are studying the matter. In any case, some level of inflation may continue during the transition phase from a bloating to a steady state economy, that is, during the course of the steady state revolution in public opinion.

Aside from inflationary concerns, saving in a pure sense is difficult logistically. If the liquidator brings the money to a traditional bank, the bank will loan it to developers. (Theoretically, nonloaning, noninvesting, purely saving banks could arise in the midst of the steady state revolution in public opinion.) If the liquidator tries to stash it at home, then personal security becomes an issue. If she tries to get the money out of circulation once and for all by shoving the damnable medium into the $30,000 marble-girded fireplace, she is breaking the law. All of this is asking too much of the liquidator.

If the liquidator has reformed to the radical point of voluntary currency destruction, there is of course the outstanding option of charity. By the giving of charity, several things may be accomplished. First, the liquidator does not wastefully consume resources. Second, supporting a charitable cause benefits society, and in that sense represents an investment in the grandkids. Third, the liquidator, and rightfully so, finds a source of self-esteem to replace that attained via conspicuous consumption.

At first glance, this third function may appear slightly anti-Christian. After all, Christian charity is supposed to be an inconspicuous affair, where the reward is obtained in heaven, not at the banquets of reformed liquidators. However, this matter is irrelevant, as it may readily be seen that the true Christian wouldn't have been a liquidator to begin with. It doesn't take a biblical scholar to recall what Jesus generally had to say about riches and liquidation. One cannot serve God and Mammon. The rich man who revels in wealth is a fool, for that very night his life may be required of him. And if any rich man has to pass through the eye of a needle to get to God's kingdom, how much harder must it be for the liquidator who flaunts his riches?

The apostle Paul passed on the parables and instead came straight to the point:

We brought nothing into this world, nor have we the power
to take anything out . . . Those who want to be rich are falling into temptation and a trap. They are letting themselves be
captured by foolish and harmful desires which drag men down
to ruin and destruction. The love of money is the root of all
evil. (1 Timothy 6:7–10)

So if you're rich, demonstrating a little charity is the least of
your worries. But no one is perfect, it's never too late, and it
doesn't seem sacrilegious to surmise that seeking some gratification and even self-esteem via charitable contribution is far less
sinful than seeking it via yacht purchasing. Even if there is some
sin involved in the transaction, sufficient charity would at least
remove the needle's eye from the path to Heaven. Furthermore,
if liquidation continues, Heaven will be inaccessible to the souls
of a great many grandkids whose existence is precluded by a diminished carrying capacity.

While charity is at the positive end of the steady state behavioral spectrum, and all kinds of purchasing activities reside in the
middle, investment is at the other end. At first this may seem
counterintuitive; purchasing a car looks to be more "consumptive" than putting the money in stocks or mutual funds. However, by investing your money, you generally enable a corporation
to increase its capital outlay. Remember land, labor, and capital,
the factors of production? Or alternatively, natural capital, labor,
and man-made capital? By investing, you finance the engine of
man-made capital that burns the grandkids' natural capital. So
exemplary steady statism precludes liquidator-scale investment.
Small-scale amounts are okay; some capital must be produced to
replace disintegrating, "entropizing" capital in a steady state econ-

omy. And of course exceptional investments, perhaps in wind power utilities or recycling firms, are very steady statish for the time being. A major advantage to investing in such firms is that they probably tend to be run by steady staters, who will in turn spend their incomes more judiciously than, for example, the executives of a luxury auto firm.

The issue of what *not* to do with savings is so important that it deserves repetition. The steady state revolution is *not* about halting conspicuous consumption for the purpose of investing on Wall Street. The steady state revolution is in sharp contrast to the message of *Luxury Fever*, in which Robert Frank (1999:107) encouraged readers, "The only required sacrifice, as we have seen, would be a very brief reduction in the rate of increase in our spending on material goods. After a short time [of investing more than we have been], we could buy even larger houses, and even more luxuriously appointed cars and appliances if we chose to." Might as well tell a heroin addict to lay off today for the sake of a bigger kick tomorrow. Even the president of the American Manufacturers Association touted a consumption tax: "The main reason of course would be a dramatic fall in the cost of capital. There are also a wide variety of other tax-overhaul proposals . . . that could contribute to higher growth rates" (Jasinowski 1998:xxix). In the steady state revolution, saving and investment are obviously very different things.

We have seen that the erstwhile liquidator may develop a sort of steady state expenditure portfolio that consists of generous doses of charity, daring amounts of nonbanked savings, inconspicuous levels of consumption, and modest amounts of conscionable investment. Theoretically, the poor fellow may be so rich to begin with that, even after diverting large proportions to charity and savings, his personal consumption expenditure remains high enough to keep him technically in the liquidating class and subject to the attendant scorn. This illustrates again why the letter of the one percent law is not as critical as the spirit thereof, and why the liquidator identification process works so readily. For although this reformer, having nowhere else to turn with the money, consumes within the upper one percentile, his consumption becomes less and less conspicuous, so that he blends in with the amorphic class. If he masters this process, he may even come to be viewed as a steady stater.

The purchasing behavior of the liquidator is important in more than just its material aspects. It also contributes psychologically to a steady state economy. While the liquidator will be pitied or repulsed in the steady state revolution in public opinion, the reformed liquidator will perhaps achieve the highest respect of all. The liquidator-turned-steady-stater will be looked up to as a model, and his or her actions will be emulated by members of all classes. That considerable portion of expenditure practiced by the amorphic class will turn steady statish, and even steady staters will find ways to trim waste out of their lifestyles. Therefore, although all consumption leads to liquidation, inconspicuous consumption, through its psychological effects, moves society in the direction of a steady state economy. In other words, if the liquidator cannot force himself to philanthropize or save to the point of reaching the technical consumption level of the amorphic or steady state class, he can still have a positive societal impact by making his remaining consumption less conspicuous.

As we have seen, there is also the likelihood that, as the steady state revolution in public opinion proceeds, the liquidator's money may accumulate more slowly. As people strive to avoid conspicuous consumption, demand will decline, production will slow, and corporate profits—from which many liquidators' wealth derives—will be reduced. This phenomenon will probably not proceed to the point where the liquidator actually has to work, but it will reduce the excessive accumulation of money, making it much easier for the liquidator to temper consumption.

One may logically ask why this process would not extend to the point whereby the liquidator *would* have to go to work. This is essentially the same question as why there would not be a full-blown, Depression-style recession.

There are at least two reasons to be sanguine about the equilibrating capabilities of a capitalist system undergoing a steady state revolution in public opinion. The first reason is best illustrated in contrast to the current condition, in which conspicuous consumption is a status symbol. In this condition, there is no upper boundary to expenditure known, or desired, by the participants. The man with the 10,000-square-foot home is likely to build a 2,000-square-foot addition for his new art collection, when he gets around to it. He may build a third home in the mountains, or install a swimming pool at the second home in the foothills. On and on the spending goes. His status in a bloating economy depends on it, while his liquidating pathology denies the need for self-actualization. In sharp contrast, there is a tangible limit to the decrease in consumption availed by the steady state revolution in public opinion. Few indeed will voluntarily take up residence in a tent to prevent the liquidation of a small house's worth of natural capital. And even those few radicals will have to eat. To procure their food, they will either have to farm or work for a wage and buy food at the grocery store. If they farm, they will need to purchase farm implements, providing retailers and capitalists with profits in the process. If they work for wages to buy groceries, profits will fall to capitalists and retailers, respectively. Financial and production services will still be required, and will still be profitable, only to a lesser extent.

There is no need to worry, therefore, that the steady state revolution in public opinion will lead to an economic collapse. At any given population level, there is clearly a lower limit to gross national product based on biophysical requirements. Furthermore, there is no reason to believe that the steady state revolution in public opinion would lead anywhere near such a lower limit. The ideal steady state economy is one in which the standard of living is high enough for all to get an education, tend to their social and spiritual needs, participate in the polity—in short, to self-actualize while living in reasonable comfort. The key distinction between a steady state economy and a bloating economy is that the former does not produce the pressure for the Smiths to exceed the Jones in terms of consumption. The same capitalist system will continue to function, just as it always has during and after minor recessions. There will be rich and poor, the inevitable stratification of capitalism and perhaps of any economic system (including the economy of nature with its carpenter ants and mountain lions). However, the distribution of wealth will be less skewed with the steady state revolution in public opinion because liquidators and amorphs will divert more of their expenditures to charities, which tend to benefit the poor.

# CONCLUSION
*Laying New Tracks*

Common sense—the working man's collection of theory—tells us that economic growth cannot continue in perpetuity. Substitutability, efficiency, and human capital all facilitate economic growth, but the employment of each is ultimately limited by laws of physics and ecology. When the biophysical limits are tested, the system starts to react with warnings like water shortages, species extinctions, and climate change. Economic growth is therefore like most other growth phenomena; it is a wonderful thing in its early stages, but its utility declines as it proceeds. At some point it becomes a bad thing—it becomes economic bloating. At that point society's grandkids depend on society to halt the process and establish a steady state economy.

Determining when that point has been reached—when economic growth has turned into economic bloating—is a task for an enlightened, participatory democracy. Enlightenment is the first step, for the participation of ignorami is likely to do more harm than good to posterity's prospects. Neoclassical economics enlightened our understanding of the growth process throughout the twentieth century, and American industry and society benefited accordingly. Unfortunately, neoclassical economics has been co-opted by a political economy that benefits from the extension of neoclassical growth theory beyond reasonable and prudent conclusions. Our industrial and political institutions are designed to react better to short-term than long-term needs, and their short-term needs are served better by a theory of economics that encourages people to liquidate massive quantities of natural capital without worrying about the consequences. So we cannot expect neoclassical economics to enlighten us on the economic processes that occur beyond the point where growth becomes bloating, or in other words where stabilization becomes the best prospect for posterity. For enlightenment, we will have to depend on ecological economics.

Ecological economics indicates that economic bloating indeed has commenced. The red flags that rise in violation of biophysical law are waving all about. To see them, one needn't travel the countryside horseback — although that certainly helps. One need only proceed to the nearest library, don the glasses of common sense, and look at some data. Data, for example, that show increasing urban acreage and decreasing wilderness acreage, increasing energy use and decreasing petroleum supplies, increasing garbage production and decreasing landfill capacity. A degree in statistics is not required to figure out the basic cause and effect relationships here. If one likes to ponder deeper relationships, one may cross-check the data on greenhouse gas emissions with temperature increases, agricultural production with soil erosion, and water consumption with water litigation. Of course, there are data that need no cross-checking to demonstrate the links between economic bloating and problematic outcomes, like lists of pollution sources or causes of species endangerment. For the ultimate cause and effect experience in common sense, one may consider the data on environmental degradation in light of the data on increasing population and per capita consumption—in light of economic bloating, in other words.

Of course, knowledge that a problem exists is only the beginning of enlightenment. Ecological economics has made some intellectual inroads into the economics of the steady state, as we saw in part 1, but there is a long way to go. The historical problems of economies, especially inflation and unemployment, will occur in stabilizing, steady state economies just as they do in growing and bloating economies. Because co-opted neoclassical economics will continue chanting for more economic growth as the solution, we will depend upon ecological economics to explore these fundamental economic problems as manifested in stabilizing and steady state economies. More important for society, however, is the fact that enlightenment is only the first step toward a steady state economy. We cannot wait for the full academic development of ecological economics to pursue a steady state economy—not if we want the grandkids to have a clean environment, sufficient natural resources, and some semblance of open space.

Given the importance of establishing a steady state economy, why should we elaborate on a social, psychological program to pursue one? Why not simply work politically to enact policies like energy taxation and consumption limits? The answer has much to do with putting the horse before the cart. In the United States of the twenty-first century, meaningful steady state policies have no chance of passing without a revolution in public opinion. Furthermore, American democracy is all about freedom, whereby unduly restrictive policy should be the last resort. Ideally, people would be free to consume as they wish. The steady state revolution in public opinion is simply the means by which people's freely developed wishes become conducive to the grandkids' welfare. As long as conspicuous or even thoughtless consumption is the status quo, we will have a bloating economy, even if there are half-hearted corrective policies developed. In part 2, therefore, we considered a social blueprint for the steady state revolution.

Part 2 supplements common sense with an evolutionary perspective and basic motivational theory. It prescribes castigation of the liquidating class, solidarity of the steady state class, and respectful patience with the amorphic class. From an evolutionary perspective, castigation of the liquidating class is carried out most effectively through the process of mate selection, because reproduction is the most powerful motivating force beyond food and security.

Solidarity of the steady state class entails not only social unity, but a particular form of individual behavior subscribed to by its members. Foremost is prudent consumption, but steady statism also includes a long list of practical activities, including recycling, self-education in ecological economics, membership in conservation organizations, writing letters to editors about growth issues, participating in electoral politics and local governance, and steering school boards that determine what schools teach about economic growth. The list of activities is dictated quite clearly by common sense.

Social revolutions commence only when urgent needs are perceived. Historically, urgency has been gauged primarily by direct and current economic welfare. Such history is consistent with evolutionary theory, Maslow's hierarchy of needs, and religious views on the weakness of the flesh. This history is disturbing in terms of the potential for ecological economics to strike a revolutionary nerve in the body politic. The American standard of living is at an all-time high (much as r-selected wildlife populations seem healthiest in the years prior to wholesale habitat liquidation). Hoping for a steady state revolution in public opinion in this environment may seem utopian to some.

On the other hand, next year may bring invincible evidence of global warming, a calamitous water shortage, or new knowledge about a widespread, insidious pollutant. In fact, when you consider the trends, doesn't our economic bloating make these types of events virtually inevitable? Doesn't common sense dictate that economic bloating is going to degrade the environment for us and even more for the grandkids?

So in this, the conclusion to my conclusion, I seek immunity from academic convention and literary formality. I request an audience with you, the reader, on a personal level, in much the way that I introduced this book. As you have probably surmised, I was not born with a silver spoon in my mouth. I have struggled to make ends meet, making mistakes and paying dues, just like most of you. But being less gregarious perhaps than the average soul, I have invested most of my time and money in education, rather than personal relationships and financial projects. At first, I obtained my education out of curiosity and to build a career in a field I enjoyed—wildlife ecology. As time went on, it dawned on me that the world had some profoundly dire problems, and I geared my education toward helping to solve them. All told, I have spent forty-six semesters in one school or another, learning facts and theories and pondering relationships among them, but never abandoning common sense. If I have come to view economic growth as economic bloating, and economic bloating as the greatest threat to posterity, I have not arrived there recklessly. Neither have I earned a Ph.D. for the sake of wealth, nor spent thousands of hours on this book for a lack of enjoyable alternatives. With a ton of sweat, a bit of blood, and even a few tears, I have purchased my chance at social exhortation.

And I register it thus: As economic bloating threatens posterity, are we to sit back and watch it happen, eating and drinking and going to car races? *Hell no! Let us fight! Fight for the grandkids!*

Let us roll up our sleeves and solidify the steady state class. Let us gain the admiration and respect of the amorphic class. Let us turn the tables and castigate the liquidating class, clearly and severely. Let us dismiss the politicians who play neoclassical growth theory for all it's worth. Let us prevent the business executives from clearing a larger corporate landscape, letting them compete instead for limited corporate turf. Let us stop the runaway train of economic bloating, lay new tracks in the right direction, and run the train at a sustainable speed.

The grandkids can take it from there.

# REFERENCES

Abernethy, V. 1991. How Julian Simon could win the bet and still be wrong. Population and Environment 13(1):3–7.

Arrow, K., B. Bolin, R. Costanza, P. Dasgupta, C. Folke, C. S. Holling, B. O. Jansson, S. Levin, K. G. Maler, C. Perrings, and D. Pimentel. 1995. Economic growth, carrying capacity, and the environment. Science 268:520–521.

Bailey, R. 1996. An environmental apocalypse is imaginary. Pages 127–134 in O. W. Markley and W. R. McCuan, eds. 21st century Earth: opposing viewpoints. Greenhaven Press, San Diego, Calif.

Barro, R. J. 1998. Determinants of economic growth: a cross-country empirical study. MIT Press, Cambridge, Mass. 145pp.

Bartlett, A. A. 1998. Reflections on sustainability, population growth, and the environment—revisited. Renewable Resources Journal 15(4):6–23.

Begon, M., J. L. Harper, and C. R. Townsend. 1996. Ecology: individuals, populations and communities. Third edition. Blackwell Science, Oxford, U.K. 1068pp.

Berger, J. J. 1997. Charging ahead: the business of renewable energy and what it means for America. University of California Press, Berkeley. 399pp.

Bernow, S., R. Costanza, H. Daly, R. DeGennaro, D. Erlandson, D. Ferris, P. Hawken, J. A. Hoerner, J. Lancelot, T. Marx, D. Norland, I. Peters, D. Roodman, C. Schneider, P. Shyamsundar, and J. Woodwell. 1998. Ecological tax reform. Bioscience 48(3): 193–196.

Berry, A. 1996. The next 500 years: life in the coming millennium. W. H. Freeman, New York, N.Y. 338pp.

Bhaskar, R. 1981. Realism. Pages 362–363 *in* W. F. Bynum, E. J. Browne, and R. Porter, eds. Dictionary of the history of science. Princeton University Press, Princeton, N.J.

Boorstin, D. J. 1983. The discoverers. Random House, New York, N.Y. 745pp.

Boughey, A. S. 1975. Man and the environment. Second edition. Macmillan Publishing, New York, N.Y. 576pp.

Boulding, K. E. 1993. The structure of a modern economy: the United States, 1929–89. New York University Press, New York, N.Y. 215pp.

Brekke, K. A. 1997. Economic growth and the environment: on the measurement of income and welfare. Hartnolls, Cornwall, U.K. 182pp.

Brown, L. R., G. Gardner, and B. Halweil. 1999. Beyond Malthus: nineteen dimensions of the population challenge. W. W. Norton, New York, N.Y. 167pp.

Brown, L. R., and J. L. Jacobson. 1987. The future of urbanization: facing the ecological and economic constraints. Worldwatch Paper 77. Worldwatch Institute, Washington, D.C. 58pp.

Brown, L. R., and E. C. Wolf. 1984. Soil erosion: quiet crisis in the world economy. Worldwatch Paper 60. Worldwatch Institute, Washington, D.C. 49pp.

Brown, M. B. 1995. Models in political economy: a guide to the arguments. Second edition. Penguin Books, New York, N.Y. 418pp.

Brown, R. H. 1994. U.S. Department of Commerce Annual Report FY 1994. U.S. Department of Commerce, Washington, D.C. 100pp.

Brownridge, D. 1990. You can't go west. Negative Population Growth, Teaneck, N.J. 8pp.

Bulloch, D. K. 1989. The wasted ocean. Lyons and Burford, New York, N.Y. 150pp.

Cameron, R. 1989. A concise economic history of the world: from paleolithic times to the present. Oxford University Press, Oxford, U.K. 454pp.

Carnes, W. S., and S. D. Slifer. 1991. The atlas of economic indicators: a market guide to market forces and the Federal Reserve. Harper-Collins, New York, N.Y. 232pp.

Cleveland, C. J., R. Costanza, C. A. S. Hall, and R. Kaufmann. 1984. Energy and the U.S. economy: a biophysical perspective. Science 225: 890–897.

Coates, J. F., and J. Jarratt. 1989. What futurists believe. Lomond Publications, Mt. Airy, Md. 340pp.

Costanza, R. 1996. The impact of ecological economics. Ecological Economics 19:1–2.

———. 1995. Economic growth, carrying capacity, and the environment. Ecological Economics 15:89–90.

———. 1994. Three general policies to achieve sustainability. Pages 392–407 *in* A. M. Jansson, M. Hammer, C. Folke, and R. Costanza, eds. Investing in natural capital. Island Press, Washington, D.C.

———. 1989. What is ecological economics? Ecological Economics 1:1–7.

Costanza, R., and H. E. Daly. 1992. Natural capital and sustainable development. Conservation Biology 6(1):37–46.

Costanza, R., and B. C. Patten. 1995. Defining and predicting sustainability. Ecological Economics 15:193–196.

Costanza, R., R. d'Arge, R. de Groot, S. Farber, M. Grasso, B. Hannon, K. Limburg, S. Naeem, R. V. O'Neill, J. Paruelo, R. G. Raskin, P. Sutton, and M. van den Belt. 1997. The value of the world's ecosystem services and natural capital. Nature 387(6630):253–260.

Cramer, G. L., and C. W. Jensen. 1994. Agricultural economics and agribusiness. Sixth edition. John Wiley and Sons, New York, N.Y. 534pp.

Cronin, H. 1991. The ant and the peacock: altruism and sexual selection from Darwin to today. Cambridge University Press, Cambridge, U.K. 490pp.

Crumpacker, D. W., S. W. Hodge, D. Friedley, and W. P. Gregg., Jr. 1988. A preliminary assessment of the status of major terrestrial and wetland ecosystems on federal and Indian lands in the United States. Conservation Biology 2(1): 103–115.

Culbertson, J. M. 1971. "Economic growth," population, and the environment. Population and Environment 11(2): 83–100.

Czech, B. 2000. Economic growth as the limiting factor for wildlife conservation. Wildlife Society Bulletin 28(1): 4–14.

Czech, B. 2000. Economic growth, ecological economics, and wilderness preservation. *In* Proceedings of the Wilderness Science in a Time of Change Conference, Missoula, Montana, May 23–27, 1999. USDA Forest Service Proceedings RMRS-P-O.

Czech, B. 2000. The importance of ecological economics to wildlife conservation. Wildlife Society Bulletin 28(1): 2–3

———. 1997. The Endangered Species Act, American democracy, and an omnibus role for public policy. Ph.D. dissertation, University of Arizona, Tucson. 294pp.

———. 1995. Ecosystem management is no paradigm shift; let's try conservation. Journal of Forestry 93(12): 17–23.

Czech, B., and P. R. Krausman. 2000. The Endangered Species Act: history, conservation biology, and political economy. Johns Hopkins University Press, Baltimore, Md.

Czech, B., and P. R. Krausman. 1999. Public opinion on endangered species conservation and policy. Society and Natural Resources 12: 469–479.

———. 1997. Distribution and causation of species endangerment in the United States. Science 277: 1116–1117.

————. 1997. Implications of an ecosystem management literature review. Wildlife Society Bulletin 25(3):667–675.

Czech, B., P. R. Krausman, and P. K. Devers. In Press. Economic associations of species endangerment causes in the United States. BioScience.

Daly, H. E. 1993. Introduction to essays toward a steady-state economy. Pages 11–50 *in* H. E. Daly and K. N. Townsend, eds. Valuing the earth: economics, ecology, ethics. MIT Press, Cambridge, Mass. 387pp.

————. 1974. The economics of the steady state. American Economics Review 64(2):15–21.

Daly, H. E., editor. 1973. Toward a steady-state economy. W. H. Freeman, San Francisco, Calif. 332pp.

Daly, H. E., and J. B. Cobb Jr. 1994. For the common good: redirecting the economy toward community, the environment, and a sustainable future. Beacon Press, Boston, Mass. 534pp.

Daly, H. E., and K. N. Townsend, editors. 1993. Valuing the earth: economics, ecology, ethics. MIT Press, Cambridge, Mass. 387pp.

Darwin, C. R. 1979. On the origin of species by means of natural selection. Avenel Books, New York, N.Y. 459pp. First published in 1859.

Deal, C. 1993. The Greenpeace guide to anti-environmental organizations. Odonian Press, Berkeley, Calif. 110pp.

Deudney, D. 1982. Space: the high frontier in perspective. Worldwatch Paper 50. Worldwatch Institute, Washington, D.C. 69pp.

Douthwaite, R. 1992. The growth illusion: how economic growth has enriched the few, impoverished the many, and endangered the planet. Council Oak Books, Tulsa, Okla. 367pp.

Dublin, M. 1991. Futurehype: the tyranny of prophecy. Penguin Books, New York, N.Y. 290pp.

Durning, A. 1992. How much is enough?: the consumer society and the future of the earth. W. W. Norton, New York, N.Y.

Ehrenfeld, D. 1992. Conservation and economic unification. Conservation Biology 6(4):483–484.

Ehrlich, P. R. 1994. Ecological economics and the carrying capacity of Earth. Pages 38–56 *in* A. M. Jansson, M. Hammer, C. Folke, and R. Costanza, eds. Investing in natural capital. Island Press, Washington, D.C.

———. 1968. The population bomb. Ballantine Books, New York, N.Y. 223pp.

Ekelund, R. B. Jr., and R. D. Tollison. 1988. Macroeconomics. Second edition. Scott, Foresman, Glenview, Ill. 592pp.

Farber, S., and R. Costanza. 1986. The economic value of wetlands systems. Journal of Environmental Management 24:41–51.

Fleischner, T. L. 1994. Ecological costs of livestock grazing in western North America. Conservation Biology 8(3):629–644.

Folke, C., A. Jansson, J. Larsson, and R. Costanza. 1996. Ecosystem appropriation by cities. Beijer Discussion Paper Series No. 86. Beijer International Institute of Ecological Economics, Stockholm, Sweden.

Fortey, R. 1998. Life: a natural history of the first four billion years of life on Earth. Alfred A. Knopf, New York, N.Y. 346pp.

Frank, R. H. 1999. Luxury fever: why money fails to satisfy in an era of excess. Free Press, New York, N.Y. 326pp.

Frank, R. H., and P. J. Cook. 1995. The winner-take-all society: why the few at the top get so much more than the rest of us. Penguin Books, New York, N.Y. 272pp.

Franklin, B. H. 1992. U.S. Department of Commerce Annual Report FY 1992. U.S. Department of Commerce, Washington, D.C. 91pp.

Frissell, C. 1993. Topology of extinction and endangerment of native fishes in the Pacific Northwest and California (U.S.A.). Conservation Biology 7(2):342–354.

Fuller, R. 1980. Inflation: the rising cost of living on a small planet. Worldwatch Paper 34. Worldwatch Institute, Washington, D.C. 48pp.

Galbraith, J. K. 1987. Economics in perspective: a critical history. Houghton Mifflin, Boston, Mass. 324pp.

————. 1984. The affluent society. Fourth edition. Houghton Mifflin, Boston, Mass. 291pp.

Gamow, G. 1965. Matter, earth, and sky. Second edition. Prentice Hall, Englewood Cliffs, N.J. 624 pp.

Georgescu-Roegen, N. 1993. The entropy law and the economic problem. Pages 75–88 *in* H. E. Daly and K. N. Townsend, eds. Valuing the earth: economics, ecology, ethics. MIT Press, Cambridge, Mass.

Glendening, P. N. 1996. Where do we grow from here? Renewable Resources Journal 14(2):20–22.

Goble, F. G. 1970. The third force: the psychology of Abraham Maslow. Grossman Publishers, New York, N.Y. 201pp.

Goeller, H. E., and A. M. Weinberg. 1976. The age of substitutability. Science 191:683–689.

Goodland, R. 1992. The case that the world has reached limits: more precisely that current throughput growth in the global economy cannot be sustained. Population and Environment 13(3):167–182.

Gowdy, J. M. 2000. Concepts and definitions of ecological economics. Wildlife Society Bulletin 28: in press.

Gowdy, J. M., and C. N. McDaniel. 1999. The physical destruction of Nauru: an example of weak sustainability. Land Economics 75(2): 333–338.

Graves, G. 1995. Pursuing excellence in water planning and policy analysis: a history of the Institute for Water Resources. Report 405-210/57652. U.S. Government Printing Office, Washington, D.C. 382pp.

Hacker, A. 1997. Money: who has how much and why? Touchstone, New York, N.Y. 254pp.

Hall, C. A. S., R. G. Pontius Jr., L. Coleman, and J. Y. Ko. 1994. The environmental consequences of having a baby in the United States. Population and Environment 15(6):505–524.

Hamrin, R. D. 1988. America's new economy: the basic guide. Franklin Watts, New York, N.Y. 484pp.

Hannon, B., R. Costanza, and R. A. Herendeen. 1986. Measures of energy cost and value in ecosystems. Journal of Environmental Economics and Management 13:391–401.

Hannon, B., R. Costanza, and R. Ulanowicz. 1991. A general accounting framework for ecological systems: a functional taxonomy for connectivist ecology. Theoretical Population Biology 40(1):78–104.

Heilbroner, R. L. 1992. The worldly philosophers: the lives, times, and ideas of the great economic thinkers. Sixth edition. Simon and Schuster, New York, N.Y. 365pp.

Heilbroner, R. L., and L. C. Thurow. 1987. Economics explained. Second edition. Simon and Schuster, New York, N.Y. 250pp.

Hern, W. M. 1993. Is human culture carcinogenic for uncontrolled population growth and ecological destruction? BioScience 43(11): 768–773.

Hirt, P. 1994. A conspiracy of optimism: management of the national forests since World War II. University of Nebraska Press, Lincoln. 416pp.

Hodgson, G. M. 1996. Economics and evolution: bringing life back into economics. University of Michigan Press, Ann Arbor. 381pp.

Jacobsen, J. L. 1983. Promoting population stabilization: incentives for small families. Worldwatch Paper 54. Worldwatch Institute, Washington, D.C. 46pp.

James, P. C. 1994. On economic growth and ecological decay. Conservation Biology 8(4):1161–1162.

Jansson, A. M., M. Hammer, C. Folke, and R. Costanza, editors. 1994. Investing in natural capital. Island Press, Washington, D.C. 504pp.

Jasinowski, J. J. 1998. Growth in the new economy. Pages xvi–xxx *in* J. J. Jasinowski, ed. The rising tide: the leading minds of business and economics chart a course toward higher growth and prosperity. John Wiley and Sons, New York, N.Y.

Johnson, W. A. 1973. The guaranteed income as an environmental measure. Pages 175–189 *in* H. E. Daly, ed. Toward a steady-state economy. W. H. Freeman, San Francisco, Calif.

Kane, H. 1993. Fish catch no longer growing. Pages 32–33 *in* L. Starke, ed. Vital signs 1993. W. W. Norton and Company, New York, N.Y.

Kemp, J. 1998. The economic growth imperative. Pages 1–17 *in* J. J. Jasinowski, ed. The rising tide: the leading minds of business and economics chart a course toward higher growth and prosperity. John Wiley and Sons, New York, N.Y.

Kerr, J. T., and D. J. Currie. 1995. Effects of human activity on global extinction risk. Conservation Biology 9(5):1528–1538.

Keynes, J. M. 1936. The general theory of employment, interest and money. Harcourt-Brace, New York, N.Y. 403pp.

Klepper, M., and R. Gunther. 1996. The wealthy 100. Citadel Press, Secaucus, N.J. 362pp.

Knight, R. L., G. N. Wallace, and W. E. Riebsame. 1995. Ranching the view: subdivisions versus agriculture. Conservation Biology 9(2): 459–461.

Krishnan, R., J. M. Harris, and N. R. Goodwin, editors. 1995. A survey of ecological economics. Island Press, Washington, D.C. 384pp.

Kuhn, T. 1996. The structure of scientific revolutions. Third edition. University of Chicago Press, Chicago, Ill. 212pp.

Kuhn, T. 1962. The structure of scientific revolutions. First edition. University of Chicago Press, Chicago, Ill. 172pp.

Lambert, R. J. 1992. Rethinking productivity: the perspective of the earth as the primary corporation. Population and Environment 13(3): 193–208.

Luke, T. W. 1995. Reproducing planet earth?: the hubris of Biosphere 2. The Ecologist 25(4):157–162.

———. 1994. Worldwatching at the limits of growth. Capitalism, Nature, and Socialism 5(2):43–63.

Lydeard, C., and R. L. Mayden. 1995. A diverse and endangered aquatic ecosystem of the southeast United States. Conservation Biology 9(4): 800–805.

Madrick, J. 1995. The end of affluence: the causes and consequences of

America's economic decline. Random House, New York, N.Y. 223pp.

Malthus, T. R. 1803. An essay on the principle of population; or, a view of its past and present effects on human happiness; with an inquiry into our prospects respecting the future removal or mitigation of the evils which it occasions. T. Bensley, London, U.K. 610pp.

Mankiw, N. G. 1992. Macroeconomics. Worth Publishers, New York, N.Y. 514pp.

Marty, M. E. 1999. Equipoise. Pages 173–191 *in* R. Rosenblatt, ed. Consuming desires: consumption, culture, and the pursuit of happiness. Island Press, Washington, D.C.

Maslow, A. H. 1954. Motivation and personality. Harper and Brothers, New York, N.Y. 411 pp.

———. 1943. A theory of human motivation. Psychological Review 50: 370–396.

McCloskey, D. N. 1998. The rhetoric of economics. Second edition. University of Wisconsin Press, Madison. 223pp.

McDaniel, C. M., and J. M. Gowdy. 2000. Paradise for sale: a parable of nature. University of California Press, Berkeley, Calif. 208pp.

Meadows, D. H. 1991. The global citizen. Island Press, Washington, D.C. 300pp.

Meffe, G. K. and C. R. Carroll. 1994. Principles of conservation biology. Sinauer Associates, Sunderland, Mass. 600pp.

Mellor, M. 1997. Women, nature and the social construction of 'economic man.' Ecological Economics 20:129–140.

Mikesell, R. F. 1995. The limits to growth: a reappraisal. Resources Policy 21(2):127–131.

Milbrath, L. W. 1989. Envisioning a sustainable society: learning our way out. State University of New York Press, Albany. 403pp.

Miller, M. H., and C. W. Upton. 1974. Macroeconomics: a neoclassical introduction. Richard D. Irwin, Homewood, Ill. 367pp.

Naisbitt, J. 1982. Megatrends: ten new directions transforming our lives. Warner Books, New York, N.Y. 290pp.

Newland, K. 1980. City limits: emerging constraints on urban growth.

Worldwatch Paper 38. Worldwatch Institute, Washington, D.C. 31pp.

Norgaard, R. B. 1990. Economic indicators of resource scarcity: a critical essay. Journal of Environmental Economics and Management 19: 19–25.

Ophuls, W. 1977. Ecology and the politics of scarcity: prologue to a political theory of the steady state. W. H. Freeman, San Francisco, Calif. 303pp.

Orr, D. W., and D. Ehrenfeld. 1995. None so blind: the problem of ecological denial. Conservation Biology 9(5):985–987.

Paepke, C. O. 1993. The evolution of progress: the end of economic growth and the beginning of human transformation. Random House, New York, N.Y. 382pp.

Patt, A. G. 1997. Economists and ecologists: different frames of reference for global climate change. Interim Report IR-97-056, International Institute for Applied Systems Analysis, Laxenburg, Austria. 29pp.

Pearce, D. W. 1992. The MIT dictionary of modern economics. Fourth edition. MIT Press, Cambridge, Mass. 474pp.

Pimentel, D., R. Harman, M. Pacenza, J. Pecarsky, and M. Pimentel. 1994. Natural resources and an optimum human population. Population and Environment 15(5):347–368.

Postel, S. 1989. Water for agriculture: facing the limits. Worldwatch Paper 93. Worldwatch Institute, Washington, D.C. 54pp.

Prugh, T., R. Costanza, J. H. Cumberland, H. Daly, R. Goodland, and R. B. Norgaard. 1995. Natural capital and human economic survival. ISEE Press, Solomons, Md. 198pp.

Quinn, J. F., and A. Hastings. 1987. Extinction in subdivided habitats. Conservation Biology 1(3):198–208.

Raven, P. H. 1990. The politics of preserving biodiversity. BioScience 40(10):769–774.

Rees, W. E. 1998. How should a parasite value its host? Ecological Economics 25:49–52.

Reidel, C. 1988. Natural resources and the environment: the challenge of economic and social development. Population and Environment 10(1):48–58.

Ricardo, D. 1821. On the principles of political economy, and taxation. Third edition. John Murray, London, U.K. 538pp.

Roan, S. 1989. Ozone crisis: the 15-year evolution of a sudden global emergency. John Wiley and Sons, New York, N.Y. 270pp.

Robinson, J. G. 1993. The limits to caring: sustainable living and the loss of biodiversity. Conservation Biology 7(1):20–28.

Rodes, B. K., and R. Odell, compilers. 1992. A dictionary of environmental quotations. Johns Hopkins University Press, Baltimore, Md. 333pp.

Rosenblatt, R., editor. 1999. Consuming desires: consumption, culture, and the pursuit of happiness. Island Press, Washington, D.C. 230pp.

Rostow, W. W. 1990. Theorists of economic growth from David Hume to the present: with a perspective on the next century. Oxford University Press, New York, N.Y. 712 pp.

Rothschild, M. 1990. Bionomics: economy as ecosystem. Henry Holt, New York, N.Y. 423pp.

Rylander, J. C. 1996. Accounting for nature: a look at attempts to fashion a "green GDP." Renewable Resources Journal 14(2):8–13.

Samuelson, R. J. 1998. Stupid students, smart economy? Washington Post, March 12, Col. 2, p. A15.

Saunders, D. A., R. J. Hobbs, and C. R. Margules. 1991. Biological consequences of ecosystem fragmentation: a review. Conservation Biology 5(1):18–32.

Schor, J. B. 1998. The overspent American: upscaling, downshifting, and the new consumer. Basic Books, New York, N.Y. 253pp.

———. 1991. The overworked American: the unexpected decline of leisure. Basic Books, New York, N.Y. 247pp.

Schumpeter, J. A. 1976. Capitalism, socialism and democracy. Fifth edition. George Allen and Unwin, London, U.K. 437pp.

Simon, J. L. 1996. The ultimate resource 2. Princeton University Press, Princeton, N.J. 734pp.

Simon, J. L., and H. Kahn. 1984. The resourceful earth: a response to Global 2000. Blackwell, Oxford, U.K. 585pp.

Smith, A. 1976. An inquiry into the nature and causes of the wealth of nations. Clarendon Press, Oxford, U.K. 1,080pp. First published in 1776.

Smith, C. L. 1994. Connecting cultural and biological diversity in restoring Northwest salmon. Fisheries 19(2):20–26.

Solow, R. M. 1988. Growth theory: an exposition. Oxford University Press, Oxford, U.K. 109pp.

————. 1974. The economics of resources or the resources of economics. American Economics Review 64(2):1–14.

Soulé, M. E. 1991. Conservation: tactics for a constant crisis. Science 253:744–750.

Stein, H., and M. Foss. 1995. The new illustrated guide to the American economy. Second edition. AEI Press, Washington, D.C. 273pp.

Stine, G. H. 1983. The hopeful future. Macmillan, New York, N.Y. 238pp.

Thorndike, J. J. 1976. The very rich: a history of wealth. American Heritage, New York, N.Y. 344pp.

Thurow, L. C. 1981. The zero-sum society: distribution and the possibilities for economic change. Penguin Books, New York, N.Y. 230pp.

Turner, B. L. 1990. The earth as transformed by human action: global and regional changes in the biosphere over the past 300 years. Cambridge University Press, New York, N.Y. 713pp.

U.S. Bureau of Labor Statistics. 1997. Consumer expenditure survey, 1994–95. U.S. Department of Labor, Bureau of Labor Statistics, Washington, D.C. 274pp.

Veblen, T. 1973. The theory of the leisure class. Houghton Mifflin, Boston, Mass. 261pp. First published in 1899.

Viederman, S. 1994. Public policy: challenge to ecological economics. Pages 467–478 *in* A. M. Jansson, M. Hammer, C. Folke, and

R. Costanza, eds. Investing in natural capital. Island Press, Washington, D.C.

Vileisis, A. 1997. Discovering the unknown landscape: a history of America's wetlands. Island Press, Washington, D.C. 433pp.

Viterito, A. 1991. Future warming for U.S. cities. Population and Environment 13(2):101–111.

Vitousek, P. M., P. R. Ehrlich, A. H. Ehrlich, and P. Matson. 1986. Human appropriation of the products of photosynthesis. BioScience 36:368–373.

Washington Post. 1996. Campaign '96: transcript of the vice presidential debate. Washington Post, October 10, 1996:A25–A28.

Weber, P. 1994. Net loss: fish, jobs and the marine environment. Worldwatch Paper 120. Worldwatch Institute, Washington, D.C. 76pp.

Weitzman, L. J. 1984. Sex-role socialization: a focus on women. Pages 157–237 in J. Freeman, ed. Women: a feminist perspective. Mayfield Publishing, Palo Alto, Calif.

Wells, M. 1992. Biodiversity conservation, affluence and poverty: mismatched costs and benefits and efforts to remedy them. Ambio 21(3): 237–243.

Willers, B. 1994. Sustainable development: a new world deception. Conservation Biology 8(4):1146–1148.

Wilson, E. O. 1998. Consilience: the unity of knowledge. Vintage Books, New York, N.Y. 367 pp.

Wong, K. 1998. Ancestral quandary: Neanderthals not our ancestors?: not so fast. Scientific American 278(1):30–32.

World Resources Institute. 1994. World resources 1994–1995: people and the environment. Oxford University Press, New York, N.Y. 400pp.

Young, J. E. 1991. Discarding the throwaway society. Worldwatch Paper 101. Worldwatch Institute, Washington, D.C. 44pp.

Zepezauer, M., and A. Naiman. 1996. Take the rich off welfare. Odonian Press, Tucson, Ariz. 191pp.

# INDEX

pesticides, 91–92
petroleum: as economic corner-
stone, 71; high consumption of
by liquidators, 135; low consumption of by steady staters,
148; as non-renewable resource,
100; sector of economy, 27–28;
as subfactor of production, 40;
wasted by car racing, 168
philanthropy (or charity), 120, 140,
171–74
philosophy, 130
Phoenix, Arizona, 3
physiocrats, 52–53, 56
Pigou, Arthur, 23
Pinchot, Gifford, 8
piss fir, 4, 39
pity, 128, 133, 145–46, 149–50,
163
policy design theory, 12–13
political economy. *See* capitalism;
democracy; socialism; steady
state economy
politicians, 21, 23–24, 26, 29, 47–
49, 114, 161, 182
pollock fishing on the Bering Sea,
6–7
pollution: accounted for in Index
of Sustainable Economic Welfare, 100; Americans' concern
about, 27; associated with race-
cars, 168; as cause of commercial
fisheries declines, 65; as cause
of species endangerment, 50; as
function of entropy, 83; as function of human municipality and
industry, 34–35, 87; as function
of technology, 91; as index of
economic bloating, 179; Julian
Simon's "reinvention" of, 68;

neoclassical perspective of, 101;
non-increasing in steady state
economy, 93; water, 34
Pope John Paul II, 164
population, human: Boulding's
thoughts about, 98–99; as component of economic bloating,
150, 179; as component of economic growth, 33; and division
of labor, 52; Ehrlich's thoughts
about, 88–90; growth of neces-
sitating efficiency, 53; influenced
by child licensing and taxes, 98–
99; and lower limit to gross national product, 176; Malthus'
thoughts about, 28, 72; Mill's
thoughts about, 94; and neoclassical economic growth theory,
94, 96; and prices, 69; Ricardo's
thoughts about, 123–24; Simon's thoughts about, 64, 70–
72, 75; stability and steady state
economy, 93–94, 98, 162; and
water needs, 33–34; wealth distribution among, 138, 148
populations, animal: growth of,
88–90, 181; and trophic levels,
56. *See also* economy of nature
posterity, Americans' concern for,
18, 38, 94, 105, 140, 177–78,
182. *See also* grandkids
power, wind, 85, 173. *See also*
energy
prices: as gauge of liquidating behavior, 167; as indicator of scarcity, 69–71, 75, 103, 124, 169;
stabilized in steady state economy, 170; as traditional concern
of economists, 29, 45
property rights, 18, 70, 81

psychology, 26, 113, 126, 129, 142,
153, 174, 179
Ptolemy, 43, 47, 79

Quesnay, François, 52

racing, car, 113, 168
radiation, nuclear, 65
Raedeke, Kenneth, 7
Ravenna Park, 74
raw materials, 28
Reagan, Ronald, 20
recession, economic, 162, 175–76.
*See also* business cycles; Great
Depression
recycling, 156, 173, 180
Red Lobster, 141
regulations, proliferating because
of economic growth, 74–75
religion, 144. *See also* Christianity;
God
reproduction, 130–34, 139
revolutions, general social, 81–82.
*See also* economics, ecological:
as social revolution; industrial
revolution; scientific revolutions; steady state revolution
revulsion (incurred by liquidating
class), 134–46
Ricardo, David, 22, 28, 123
rigor trap, 88, 141
risk, 38, 68, 115–16
River of No Return Wilderness,
4
robins, 129
Rongstad, Orin, 11, 13
Roosevelt, Franklin, 29–30
Roosevelt, Theodore, 8
r-selection, 89–90, 112
Ruby Valley, Nevada, 2

Salvi, Joe, 2
Samuelson, Robert J., 19
San Carlos Apache Reservation,
10–12, 126
San Carlos Apache Tribe, 10–12
San Pedro River, Arizona 2
saving (of money), 166, 170–71,
173–74
Say's law, 30
Schumpeter, Joseph, 82
scientific method, 35, 80
scientific revolutions, 47–48, 79
Seattle, Washington, 7, 34, 74, 137
self-actualization, 126, 130–31,
142–46, 154, 156, 164, 175–76
self-esteem, 126–33, 139, 143,
149, 171–72
services sector, 51–61. *See also* "information economy"
Simon, Julian, 61–77, 85, 100, 103,
161
slavery, 110
Smith, Adam, 22–23, 28, 30, 60
socialism, 74, 111
Solow, Robert, 76–77, 96
Sonoran Desert, 3, 10
Soylent Green, 97
space, outer, 36, 44
space travel, 44
spending: on construction, 134;
correlated with income, 139;
liquidating propensity of, 166–
67; on public works during New
Deal, 29–30; related to investment, 173; stigmatized during
steady state revolution, 170; on
unnecessary goods and services,
112–13, 175. *See also* consumption, per capita; personal consumption expenditure